The Fullness of the Spirit

by

William M. Greathouse

Beacon Hill Press of Kansas City
Kansas City, Missouri

Copyright, 1958
By Nazarene Publishing House

ISBN 083-412-1441

Printed in the United States of America

22 21 20 19 18

To Ruth

Introduction

Someone has said that the Holy Spirit is the unknown person of the Trinity. It is probably true that all too frequently when Protestants recite that portion of the creed, "I believe in the Holy Spirit," they thereby exhaust their knowledge and vocabulary concerning the Spirit.

Here is a delightful book by Dr. William M. Greathouse on this pertinent theme that is both fresh and fragrant. Its charm lies in its readableness and simplicity; its strength is in its theological soundness and clarity of thought; and its appeal lies in its pertinency for all Christians in our day.

The book itself was written originally as a class book for lay instruction. It is scholarly, but never stilted or bookish, and its widely drawn illustrations have a universal appeal. I predict that this book will have a wide distribution in many circles where there is a sincere desire to know the Holy Spirit in His fullness in personal redemption.

—Samuel Young

Contents

Preface

The late General Superintendent Roy T. Williams would frequently admonish candidates for the ministry, "Honor the Blood; honor the Holy Ghost." The purpose of this little volume can be stated quite simply—to honor the Holy Spirit.

It is true, the Spirit does not seek honor. There is about Him "an incurable tendency to self-effacement." Jesus declared: "When he, the Spirit of truth, is come, . . . he shall not speak of himself; . . . he shall glorify me" (John 16:13-14). It is His work to exalt our Lord Jesus Christ. Nevertheless, this is the peculiar era of the Holy Spirit. At Pentecost He was "given" to the Church, and through the Church to the world. In the economy of God He is the Agent of personal salvation in this Pentecostal era. All God does *in* man He does by the Spirit. He is God at work in the inner recesses of human personality. Therefore it is important that we trace as best we can the office work of the Third Person of the adorable Trinity.

The crowning work of the Holy Spirit is entire sanctification or Christian perfection. The distinguishing tenet within the Wesleyan tradition is the teaching that through the Gift of the Holy Spirit in Pentecostal fullness the heart of the Christian believer is made pure from sin and perfect in love. By this Gift he is also empowered for effective Christian service and for personal witnessing. If the precious doctrine of entire sanctification is to be kept vital and virile, the Holy Spirit must be honored in our thought and experience. "Beliefs seldom become doubts; they become ritual." They die, and we safely embalm them in creed and ritual. *The surest safeguard against this threat is complete openness to the Spirit.* This book will have served its purpose if it helps in any degree to create such a concern, such a sensitivity to the Holy Spirit. The author makes no claim to originality or exhaustiveness of treatment. His aim is solely to suggest and to sensitize.

The following publishers have kindly granted permission to use copyrighted materials: Abingdon Press, quotations from E. Stanley Jones, *Victorious Living* and *Abundant Living;* Broadman Press, quotation from W. T. Conner, *The Work of the Holy Spirit;* Christian Publications, Inc., quotation from A. B. Simpson, *Power from on High;* Wm. B. Eerdmans Publishing Co., quotation from F. F. Bruce, *Commentary on the Book of Acts;* Harper and Brothers, quotations from J. S. Bonnell, *Psychology for Pastor and People,* from Fenelon, *Christian Perfection,* from C. W. Lowry, *The Trinity and Christian Devotion;* Macmillan and Company, quotation from J. B. Phillips, *Letters to Young Churches;* Fleming Revell Co., quotations from Samuel Chadwick, *The Way to Pentecost,* and from R. A. Torrey, *The Holy Spirit;* the Standard Press, quotation from J. A. Huffman, *The Holy Spirit;* the Westminster Press, quotation from George S. Hendry, *The Holy Spirit in Christian Theology.* The author is indebted to many other works on the Holy Spirit not here acknowledged by name.

A special word of appreciation is due to Dr. Kenneth S. Rice, director of Christian Service Training, and to Rev. Norman R. Oke, book editor of the Nazarene Publishing House, for valuable counsel and supervision in the preparation of this text, and to the Christian Service Training Commission for extending to me the honor of preparing this Golden Anniversary text on this most sacred theme.

WILLIAM M. GREATHOUSE

I

Life in the Spirit

If we live in the Spirit, let us also walk in the Spirit (Gal. 5:25).

Dr. D. I. Vanderpool was concluding a sermon to the student body of a Christian college. "It is wonderful to be born of the Spirit and filled with the Spirit," he said; "but it is just as wonderful—and fully as important—that we learn to *live* and *walk* in the Spirit." Then he asked his listeners, "Now that you are saved and sanctified, what are you going to do about it?"

Dr. Vanderpool was emphasizing the cardinal truth that life in the Spirit is conditional upon an unfolding consecration, obedience, and trust. Dr. J. B. Chapman used to stress that the Spirit's presence in our lives is analogous to the light that fills a room at night. The light is present so long as the conditions obtain which make light possible. For this reason he urged that we think of the *condition* rather than the *state* of holiness. John put it unforgettably: "If we walk in the light, as he is in the light, we have fellowship one with another, and the blood of Jesus Christ his Son cleanseth us from all sin" (I John 1:7).

The two initial crises of Christian experience are essential to spiritual life. The unconverted man must be born anew before he can have life in God. The justified man must be baptized with the Holy Spirit if he is to know the fullness of life. To be regenerated and sanctified wholly is to *live* in the Spirit; but "if we live in the Spirit, let us also *walk* in the Spirit." It is imperative that we cultivate the fellowship of the Holy Spirit. Ceasing from self-effort, we must learn to live and work in the power of the indwelling Comforter. Yielding ourselves moment by moment to His lordship, we must learn what it is to live a Spirit-controlled life. Sensing our dependence upon Him, we must discover the privilege of being led by the Spirit. Recognizing our spiritual poverty apart from Him, we must learn to pray in the Spirit. Keeping our hearts open to His tender searching, we must permit Him to examine our lives, to prune and cultivate them, that we may bring forth the fruit of the Spirit.

What are the characteristics of life in the Spirit? A complete answer to this question would carry us far beyond the limits of this small book, for the Spirit-filled life is a diamond of many facets. We shall view it from four angles.

A. A Life of Assurance

One of the deepest longings of the human spirit is the yearning to be accepted. Life becomes almost intolerable unless we know the security of love; but if we know that someone genuinely cares for us, we can bear almost anything. When that One is God, life has found its ultimate security and peace. John Wesley relates an experience many of us can understand. "In the evening I went very unwillingly to a society in Aldersgate Street," he writes in his *Journal* on May 24, 1738, "where one was reading Luther's preface to the *Epistle to the Romans.* About a quarter before nine, while he was describing the change which God works in the heart through faith in Christ, I felt my heart strangely warmed. I felt I did trust in Christ, Christ alone for salvation; and an assurance was given me that He had taken away *my* sins, even *mine,* and saved *me* from the law of sin and death." This testimony has become classic. It is important because it indicates something of the nature of Christian assurance.

1. *The Witness of the Spirit.* The Word declares: "The Spirit himself beareth witness with our spirit, that

we are the children of God" (Rom. 8:16, ASV). It is difficult to explain to one who has not experienced it just what we mean by the witness of the Spirit. Bernard of Clairvaux put it poetically: "The love of Jesus, what it is, none but His loved ones know." But with Mr. Wesley perhaps we can say the witness is "an inward impression on the soul, whereby the Spirit of God immediately and directly witnesses to my spirit, that I am a child of God, that Jesus Christ hath loved me, and given Himself for me; that all my sins are blotted out, and *I*, even *I*, am reconciled to God."[1] The earnest penitent who looks to Christ comes to the place of inward release and conscious acceptance with God. "He that believeth on the Son of God hath the witness in himself" (I John 5:10). Beyond this it is hard to go. Paul phrased it beautifully in Galatians: "And because ye are sons, God hath sent forth the Spirit of his Son into your hearts, crying, Abba, Father" (Gal. 4:6). By the Spirit of adoption the pardoned sinner is enabled to look up to God and say, "Father!" This is the *direct* witness of the Spirit.

To the direct witness of the Holy Spirit there is added the *indirect* witness of one's own spirit. The Spirit of God bears "witness *with* our spirit." There is a joint witness of His Spirit and mine that I have passed from condemnation to acceptance and sonship. This indirect witness confirms the direct, assuring me that I am not presuming upon God. By my own spirit I perceive that I am a new creature in Christ. "Old things are passed away; behold, all things are become new." *This I know.*

To the man born blind the Pharisees put questions he could not answer. But he could not be silenced! "One thing I know," he said, "that, whereas I was blind, now I see." Stubborn fact! Yes, and we have the same kind of indisputable evidence if we have met the Christ. "For God, who commanded the light to shine out of darkness,

[1]*Sermons,* "Witness of the Spirit: II," II, 2.

hath shined in our hearts, to give the light of the knowledge of the glory of God in the face of Jesus Christ" (II Cor. 4:6). I came to Jesus and I found—light, peace, release from my sins! "Hereby we do know that we know him, if we keep his commandments" (I John 2:3). "We know that we have passed from death unto life, because we love the brethren" (I John 3:14). "And hereby we know that we are of the truth, and shall assure our hearts before him" (I John 3:19).

There is, moreover, the same twofold witness to our entire sanctification. "But how do you know that you are sanctified, saved from your inbred corruption?" Mr. Wesley asks. "I can know it no otherwise than I know that I am justified. 'Hereby know we that we are of God,' in either sense, 'by the Spirit that he hath given us.' We know by the *witness* and by the *fruit* of the Spirit."[2]

He goes on to point out that the witness is not always the same, in justification or in sanctification. Sometimes it is clear and distinct; at other times it is fainter. "And sometimes it is withdrawn. Yet, in general, the latter testimony of the Spirit is as clear and as steady as the former." The consecrated Christian must await this witness in joyful expectancy, not straining, but resting, fully confident that the Spirit will come and make himself known—in His own way. "The Lord, whom ye seek, shall suddenly come to his temple." The witness is often accompanied by ecstasy, which in time becomes peaceful love. When the Spirit comes to abide, the overflow of His indwelling is rivers of Christlike love. "We know by the witness and by the fruit of the Spirit."

2. *The Seal of the Spirit.* In II Corinthians we encounter a kindred truth, that God "hath also sealed us, and given the earnest of the Spirit in our hearts" (II Co

[2]*A Plain Account of Christian Perfection,* p. 25.

1:22). This is a thrilling and precious truth. Letters and all kinds of official documents were in those days sealed with wax. A warm blob of wax was placed upon the letter or document; the sender or signer then pressed his signet into the wax, making an official seal. *The Holy Spirit in the believer's life is the divine seal of approval upon that life.* "The foundation of God standeth sure, having this seal, The Lord knoweth them that are his. And, Let every one that nameth the name of Christ depart from iniquity" (II Tim. 2:19). If the submissive heart is the warm and plastic wax, the Holy Spirit is the Sealer—and the image of Christ is the visible mark of identification. The seal is at once an assurance to the believer and a sign to the world. Some question whether one can know himself entirely sanctified, on the grounds that no man can know the hidden depths of his own heart. *But God knows.* "And God, which knoweth the hearts, bare them witness, giving them the Holy Ghost . . . purifying their hearts by faith" (Acts 15:8, 9). "The seal of God standeth sure."

The metaphor of the *earnest* suggests another beautiful truth. The earnest is a partial payment which binds the bargain and obliges both buyer and seller to complete the transaction. The gift of the Holy Spirit is the first installment, as it were, of the infinite treasure God plans to bestow upon us in heaven. So long as we walk in the Spirit we have the *guarantee,* plus the *foretaste,* of heaven. This is conditional, to be sure, upon our continuing to walk in the light; but so long as the Spirit abides and the seal remains unbroken, we have the assurance of heaven. Eternal life is not merely future; it is a present experience which reaches into eternity.

Blessed assurance, Jesus is mine!
Oh, what a foretaste of glory divine!

What will heaven be? It will be the fulfillment of the love, joy, and peace we now know in Christ—lifted to infinity! "This is life eternal, that they might know thee the only true God, and Jesus Christ, whom thou hast sent" (John 17:3). Heaven is not essentially jasper walls and golden streets—heaven is God. To know Him is to experience a foretaste of heaven. Paul calls this the earnest of the Spirit. (See Eph. 1:13-14.)

B. A Spirit-controlled Life

We turn the diamond about now to view another facet: "The fruit of the Spirit is . . . self-control" (Gal. 5:22-23, ASV). As glorious as is the experience of perfect love, "we have this treasure in earthen vessels" (II Cor. 4:7). And we cannot lose sight of this fact without destroying the beautiful symmetry of Bible holiness. The Holy Spirit sanctifies, but does not cancel, our human nature. "For the Son of man is not come to destroy men's lives, but to save them" (Luke 9:56). How shall we understand this?

The Book of Genesis discloses to us that man in God's image was holy. His life was ordered and harmonious, whole and integrated. Living in perfect communion with God, his entire life was under the sanctifying control of the Spirit of God. But something has happened to human nature. By the Fall man forfeited the gift of the Holy Spirit—the glory departed. As a consequence, man's lower nature—his selfish and sensual impulses—came to dominate his spirit. Cut off from God, man became a creature of the flesh. His life had known a beautiful God-centeredness; it now festered in ugly self-centeredness.

It is the work of the Holy Spirit to restore the original order and harmony of human nature. This does not mean that we are brought back to Adamic perfection, for our humanity bears the marks of sin's racial history. Only the stroke of omnipotence at the second coming of Christ can erase the effects of sin from human nature. But by the gift of the Spirit in this age we can be changed from self-centered to God-centered persons. By the regenerating and sanctifying grace of the Holy Spirit our disordered, corrupt human nature can be restored to Christlike order and beauty. By the indwelling of the Holy Spirit my entire selfhood is brought once more under the sway of God. "For what the law could not do, in that it was weak through the flesh, God sending his own Son in the likeness of sinful flesh, and for sin, condemned sin in the flesh; that the righteousness of the law might be fulfilled in us, who walk not after the flesh, but after the Spirit. So then they that are in the flesh cannot please God. But ye are not in the flesh, but in the Spirit, if so be that the Spirit of God dwell in you. . . . For if ye live after the flesh, ye shall die: but if ye through the Spirit do mortify the deeds of the body, ye shall live" (Rom. 8:3-4, 8-9, 13). *In the body but not in the flesh* —this is not said to the saints in heaven but to the saints in Rome!

Meaning of "Flesh"

Now as long as we shall live in this body we shall experience some tension between the spirit and the body. This tension is a part of our probationary existence, and it is essential to the development of faith and holiness. As a mature saint, Paul wrote, "But I keep under my body, and bring it into subjection: lest that by any means, when I have preached to others, I myself should be a castaway" (I Cor. 9:27). And James cautions us that one form of temptation consists in the arousing of desire (Jas. 1:13-14). This temptation is the suggestion that we gratify a normal desire out of harmony with God's will, and it often succeeds in awakening a response from the appetitive nature. This, however, is not necessarily sin. Sin enters only when the will gives its consent. So long as I say *No,* I have not sinned. "Yield not to temptation, for *yielding is sin.*" But caution! Imagination versus will is an uneven battle. What gets your imagination eventually gets you; therefore your safety lies in turning to Christ immediately.

Our appetites, we conclude, are blind and unreasoning. They know no right or wrong—they simply clamor for satisfaction. But God has given us reason to control desire, and the sanctified man is no exception to this rule. The consecrated person, however, has shut the door of his life to sin; he has put on the Lord Jesus Christ and thus makes no provision for the flesh (Rom. 13:14). "They that are Christ's have crucified the flesh with the affections and lusts" (Gal. 5:24). He fills his mind with those things which are "true," "honest," "just," "pure," "lovely, and "of good report" (Phil. 4:8). *But in addition to this he lives in the power of the indwelling Spirit.* By that power he is able to resist every temptation and glorify God in his body. This is the revealed secret of holy living.

By the *flesh,* however, the New Testament means more than untrammeled desire. Some of the most telling traits of carnality are sins of selfishness: envy, pride, jealousy, anger, and such (I Cor. 3:1-4; Gal. 5:20-21). Not only must we mortify the impulses of our bodies; we must keep our natural self-love in check by walking in the Spirit. Jesus said, "Thou shalt love thy neighbour *as thyself.*" By nature we love ourselves excessively. Likening human nature to a pair of scales, we may say that apart from God's grace we are heavily weighted and tipped toward self. We may jump up and down in the scales and move them somewhat, but by our own efforts we can never achieve a balance between self and others! *However, by the gift of the Spirit, GOD lays His hand on the scales of life and brings them to a balance!* To maintain this balance we must "walk in the Spirit." But as we so walk, "the love of God is shed abroad in our hearts by the Holy Ghost," and we are enabled to keep the second great commandment.

We believe, therefore, that the Scriptures teach both *eradication* and *self-discipline*—the radical cleansing from sin and the discipline of our legitimate selfhood. The two truths are not contradictory but complementary.

C. A Life of Fellowship

In pronouncing his benediction upon the Corinthians, Paul speaks of "the communion of the Holy Ghost" (II Cor. 13:14). This phrase suggests one of the most sacred and precious aspects of the Spirit-filled life. Can anything be more glorious than the indwelling of God within my personality? The Shekinah of God within my breast! How I must cherish His presence and cultivate His fellowship! How careful I must be never to grieve Him or quench His love! At whatever cost, I must maintain the peace of God within the citadel of my soul.

1. *Led by the Spirit.* "As many as are led by the Spirit of God, they are the sons of God" (Rom. 8:14).

Guide me, O Thou great Jehovah,
Pilgrim through this barren land!

If some of us in our zeal tend to get ahead of Him, others of us are in danger of lagging behind. We should endeavor to live where we can hear the smallest whisper of His voice. When Dr. E. Stanley Jones was elected bishop of the Methodist church, the Inner Voice whispered, "I want you in India." And Dr. Jones declined the highest honor his church could confer upon him. Sometimes it is not so easy to get His signals—then we must pray until the clamor of human desire subsides. But how sweet to know—and obey! At times, however, we may fail completely to discover that inner direction. What then? We may then safely seek the counsel of spiritually-minded friends who can survey our situation objectively. The Spirit often guided the apostles through others who were acquainted with His ways (Acts 11:28-30; 21:10-11, *et al.*). There are occasions even when it would appear God leaves us to make our own decisions. As a wise parent delights in the maturing judgment of his son, so our Heavenly Father rejoices in our sanctified choices. But even in these choices we are being *indirectly* guided by the Spirit as we seek to make only those choices which would glorify God.

There is another important phase of the Spirit's leadership: He guides us into the truth as it is in Jesus (John 6:13). This is of deep significance in the cultivation of Christian character. One of our most urgent needs is to find the secret of emotional stability. Actually, healthy emotion is a by-product of something deeper.

> Truths seen and realized through the aid of the Holy Spirit bring a glow of feeling. When the truth becomes familiar the glow of feeling is likely to subside or fade in consciousness. The result of the ebb and flow of emotional experience has often been an occasion of difficulty for young and inexperienced Christians. Many have unwisely sought for religious feeling as such. The essential factor, however, in the development of the emotional life of the Christian is to search the Word for new truth, or plead the Spirit's guidance into the deeper aspects of truth already known. Feeling apart from truth leads into dangerous fanaticism, but truth which gives rise to strong emotion becomes a supreme power in the life of holiness.[3]

We need not doubt the faithfulness of the Spirit to help us at this point. Jesus assures us that "when he, the Spirit of truth, is come, he will guide you into all truth."

2. *Praying in the Spirit.* The discovery of a satisfactory prayer life is another essential to holy living. But, thank God, "the Spirit also helpeth our infirmities: for we know not what we should pray for as we ought: but the Spirit itself maketh intercession for us with groan-

[3]Wiley and Culbertson, *Introduction to Christian Theology* (Kansas City: Beacon Hill), p. 355.

ings which cannot be uttered. And he that searcheth the hearts knoweth what is the mind of the Spirit, because he maketh intercession for the saints according to the will of God" (Rom. 8:26-27). Is this what Jude meant by "praying in the Holy Ghost" (Jude 20)? The writer must confess that he knew little of a rich and satisfying prayer life until the Comforter came to abide. Then to his amazement he found a window of his soul opening toward Jerusalem! Commenting on Paul's assertion in Romans, Dr. J. A. Huffman says: "Whether the inexpressible or word-baffling groanings [are those of the human spirit, superinduced by the Holy Spirit, or whether they are the groanings] of the Holy Spirit, himself, the result of the intercession is, that the burden, the longing, the sighs, the groans, the tears are borne effectually to the throne of grace, and there are translated into an intelligent petition before God."[4] Prayer keeps the channel open for the inflow of the Spirit.

3. *Being Filled with the Spirit.* Paul exhorts the Romans to "maintain the spiritual glow" (Rom. 12:11*b*, Moffatt). To the Ephesians he writes, "Be filled with the Spirit" (Eph. 5:18). This latter exhortation reads literally, "Keep on being filled with the Spirit." We must keep the springs of the Spirit unclogged. But sometimes in the stress of living the ardor of our devotion tends to cool; then we need to pray through to a new anointing. We must reckon with the ebb and flow of emotion, the effects of illness and disappointment, and a thousand other infirmities of the flesh. There are even periods of spiritual dryness when God seems to withdraw himself from us to test the mettle of our devotion. Because we have this treasure in earthen vessels we must experience repeated renewals of the Spirit. We must, at whatever

[4]*The Holy Spirit* (Winona Lake, Ind.: The Standard Press), p. 147.

cost, maintain spiritual reality. Again and again we must break through to newness in God.

Spirit of the living God, fall fresh on me!
Break me, melt me, mold me, fill me—
Spirit of the living God, fall fresh on me!

4. *Living in the Power of the Indwelling Comforter.* For several years the writer lived an unsatisfactory Christian life. With sincerity of purpose and resolution of will he endeavored to live a consecrated, Christlike life. But it was as if he were trying to operate in his own power. Then one day he honestly faced himself and acknowledged that he did not have the reserve power of the Holy Spirit of which he had heard others tell. With hungry heart he began to read the words of Jesus in the fourteenth chapter of John: "If ye love me, keep my commandments. And I will pray the Father, and he shall give you another Comforter, that he may abide with you for ever; even the Spirit of truth; whom the world cannot receive, because it seeth him not, neither knoweth him: but ye know him; for he dwelleth with you, and shall be in you. . . . and he that loveth me shall be loved of my Father, and I will love him, and will manifest myself to him" (John 14:15-17, 21). Somewhere along in this wondrous passage his heart began to burn within him—with an intuitive awareness he knew that the Holy Spirit had come in person to abide! The faith to appropriate was given almost unconsciously, but *the Comforter had come.* Instantly a new door opened into the holiest of all. Futility was swallowed up in fullness, impotence in power. Since that glorious day his life has known a new level of victory. For it is "not by might, nor by power, but by my spirit, saith the Lord of hoses" (Zech. 4:6). "We which have believed do enter into rest . . . There remaineth therefore a rest to the people of God. For he that is entered into his rest, he also hath

ceased from his own works, as God did from his" (Heb. 4:3, 9-10).

Thomas Cook tells of a young bride who found that everything she tried to do in the home went wrong. She did her best, but such difficulties arose that she was almost in a state of despair. One day she was so discouraged she sat down and wept. She was aroused by a knocking at the door, and found a telegraph boy with a telegram announcing that her mother was coming—and immediately her care was gone. "When Mother arrived," she said, "I had no more anxiety. What I could not do Mother could, and when she was with me, I rested." "Casting all your care upon him, for he careth for you" (I Pet. 5:7).

Yes, 'tis sweet to trust in Jesus,
Just from sin and self to cease;
Just from Jesus simply taking
Life and rest, and joy and peace.
—LOUISA M. R. STEAD

D. A LIFE OF FRUITFULNESS

When God called Abram, He said to him, "I will bless thee . . . and thou shalt be a blessing" (Gen. 12:2). He does not bestow His grace upon us that we may exploit it selfishly. No, He blesses us that we might in turn be a blessing to others. "I am the true vine," says Jesus, "and my Father is the husbandman. Every branch in me that beareth not fruit he taketh away: and every branch that beareth fruit, he purgeth it, that it may bring forth more fruit. Herein is my Father glorified, that ye bear much fruit; so shall ye be my disciples" (John 15:1-2, 8). There is no mistaking it, "By their fruits ye shall know them" (Matt. 7:20).

When the Holy Spirit comes in His fullness, our natural powers are vitalized, our dormant capacities are quickened, our human capabilities are reinforced. The mind receives a new alertness of understanding and keenness of insight. The heart finds a new simplicity of motive and intensity of devotion. We begin to become effective for God.

This, however, is a problem area for many sincere Christians. They have preconceived ideas of how the Spirit of God will use them. They expect to be endowed with marvelous and miraculous powers for service and soul winning. They have heard how God has turned commonplace persons into marvels of power, and they look in vain for the same results in their own lives. Thus they are thrown into confusion and distress. Such persons need to be reminded that there is a fundamental difference between the *gifts* and the *fruit* of the Spirit.

1. *The Gifts of the Spirit.* "Now there are diversities of gifts," says Paul, "but the same Spirit. And there are differences of administration, but the same Lord. And there are diversities of operations, but it is the same God which worketh all in all. But the manifestation of the Spirit is given to every man to profit withal" (I Cor. 12:4-7). Two truths here call for elaboration.

There is a manifold variety in the gifts of the Spirit. To each is given the manifestation of the Spirit for the common good. Although it is "to every man according to his several ability" (Matt. 25:15), these are gifts of the *Spirit.* God bestows in line with our natural aptitudes, however, and we have varying capabilities. "I cannot teach a Sunday school class," a good woman once testified in prayer meeting, "but how I enjoy knocking on doors and inviting people to church!" To each his gift, as God wills. The baptism with the Spirit does not make everyone a flaming evangelist. "He gives the Spirit to some that they may be ministers of helpfulness; to some that they may be faithful witnesses; and to others that they may be sanctified mothers who are keepers at home and miracles of patience, wisdom, and sweetness. To each there is a gift of the Spirit, and whatever the kind of gift, there is to all the gift of power for effective service and testimony."[5] A mother with ten children wrote the great Gypsy Smith to tell him that God had called her to preach. "You are to be congratulated," Smith wrote in reply to her letter, "first, that He has called you to preach; secondly, that He has furnished you with a congregation!"

There is a divine purpose in the gifts of the Spirit. A gift is a supernatural endowment for service to the body of Christ. As in the human body there are many members, so in the Church there are diversities of gifts, for the edification of the body of Christ. The Corinthians were rich in gifts but scandalously carnal! Their gifts became a source of rivalry, jealousy, pride, and disorder in worship. With all charity we must say that the Corinthians are still with us. They are those who equate emotionalism with spirituality and who fail to perceive the distinction between the *gifts* and the *fruit* of the Spirit. Gifts are bestowed for one purpose only: for service to the Church. The greater the service, the more important the gift.

2. *The Fruit of the Spirit.* If gifts are for service, fruit is for character. Gifts are functional; fruit is a quality of life. The final proof that we are possessed and indwelt by the Holy Spirit is the beauty and power of Christlike love subduing and sanctifying us.

"This love of which I speak is slow to lose patience—it looks for a way of being constructive. It is not possessive: it is neither anxious to impress nor does it cherish inflated ideas of its own importance.

"Love has good manners and does not pursue selfish advantage. It is not touchy. It does not compile statistics

[5]Chadwick, *The Way to Pentecost* (New York: Revell, 1940), p. 106.

of evil or gloat over the wickedness of other people. On the contrary, it is glad with all good men when Truth prevails.

"Love knows no limit to its endurance, no end to its trust, no fading of its hope: it will outlast anything. It is, in fact, the only thing that stands when all else has fallen."[6]

Or, as Paul puts it in Galatians, "The fruit of the Spirit is love, joy, peace, longsuffering, gentleness, goodness, faith, meekness, temperance" (Gal. 5:22-23). Observe that the word "fruit" is singular. The number is plural but the grammar is correct—for each fruit is a manifestation of LOVE. Joy is love exulting in God. Peace is love resting in God. Long-suffering, gentleness, and meekness are love subduing our spirits and making them like the Saviour. Faith is love clinging to God. Temperance is love controlling the entire being.

> In newspaper English, the passage would read something like this: The Fruit of the Spirit is an affectionate, lovable disposition, a radiant spirit and a cheerful temper, a tranquil mind and a quiet manner, a forbearing patience in provoking circumstances and with trying people, a sympathetic insight and tactful helpfulness, generous judgment and a big-souled charity, loyalty and reliableness under all circumstances, humility that forgets self in the joy of others, in all things self-mastered and self-controlled, which is the final mark of perfecting.[7]

"Love," said John Wesley, "is the highest gift of God—humble, gentle, patient love. . . . There is nothing higher in religion; there is, in effect, nothing else; if you look for anything but more love, you are looking wide of the mark, you are getting out of the royal way. And when you are asking others, Have you received this or that blessing? if you mean anything but more love you

[6]I Corinthians 13:4-7, Phillips. *Letters to Young Churches* (New York: The Macmillan Co.).

[7]Chadwick, *op. cit.*, p. 104.

are wrong; you are leading them out of the way, and putting them upon a false scent. *Settle it then in your heart, that from the moment God has saved you from sin you are to aim at nothing more, but more of that love described in the thirteenth of the First Epistle to the Corinthians.*"[8]

Gracious Spirit, Holy Ghost,
Taught by Thee, we covet most,
Of Thy gifts at Pentecost,
Holy, heavenly love.
—CHRISTOPHER WORDSWORTH (1807-85)

Questions for Discussion

1. Explain the two phases of the witness of the Spirit (*a*) in relation to the new birth, (*b*) in relation to entire sanctification.

2. What is the significance of (*a*) the seal of the Spirit? (*b*) the earnest of the Spirit?

3. Show the relationship between self-discipline and eradication.

4. Should a Christian ever make a decision without the direct guidance of the Spirit? Explain.

5. What dangers should we avoid in thinking of repeated fillings of the Spirit in the sanctified life?

6. What is the difference between the gifts and the fruit of the Spirit? Why is this distinction important?

[8]*A Plain Account of Christian Perfection*, p. 46.

II

The Fullness of the Spirit

Have ye received the Holy Ghost since ye believed? (Acts 19:2)

Footsore and weary, the little party finally arrived in Ephesus. For days they had been trudging along the busy highway traveled each year by thousands of pilgrims to this great center of religious interest. The towering figure in that little traveling group was the grizzled veteran from Tarsus, Paul, the apostle. For him this was a climactic day. For years he had been waiting for God to give him the green light to evangelize this great center of Asia Minor. Now he had finally arrived to launch his "Operation Christianity."

Soon he found a little handful of disciples and greeted them cordially. Now what would be his first instructions to them? What would be his words of comfort? We are amazed! He doesn't talk about statistics; he does not discuss conditions of the times; he doesn't say a thing about finance. The first words are a question—the question that burns from the very heart of the apostle and must have burned into the thinking of the disciples of Ephesus. "Have ye received the Holy Ghost since ye believed?"

This question underscores the theme of the Acts. Luke opens this book with the statement: "The former treatise have I made, O Theophilus, of all that Jesus *began* both to do and teach." The author would have us to understand that Jesus' earthly life and ministry were but the beginning of His personal activity. The ministry which our Lord began in the days of His flesh He is now *continuing* through His new body, the Spirit-filled Church. For this reason Acts has been properly called by some the *Acts of the Holy Spirit.* Within the few pages of this earliest church history we are confronted by no less than fifty-seven references to the Spirit; the entire book is a commentary on the person and work of the Holy Spirit.

A. The Secret of His Fullness

The Book of Acts is the breathtaking account of the beginning and spread of the Christian Church. Here we have a historical event that cannot be accounted for on the basis of naturalistic causes. These Nazarenes had few earthly assets. Their leader confessed, "Silver and gold have I none." They had no church edifices or salaried ministry. Most of their preachers had had no formal training for the ministry. Public opinion was all against them from the outset and opposition steadily mounted as the movement grew. One after another of their leaders was arrested and imprisoned; some were even executed. Yet in spite of all these adverse conditions, within a few years they were beginning to turn "the world upside down"—or right side up! What was the secret of this unbelievable success? You are right—these Christians were filled with the Holy Spirit. "They were all filled with the Holy Ghost, *and began . . .*" (Acts 2:4).

1. *The Command of Christ.* Luke is careful to give us the setting for this unprecedented spiritual movement. Before His ascension Christ gathered His disciples about Him on Mount Olivet. "Being assembled together with them, [he] commanded them that they should not depart from Jerusalem, but wait for the promise of the Father, which, saith he, ye have heard of me. For John truly baptized with water; but ye shall be baptized with the Holy Ghost not many days hence" (Acts 1:4-5). They must "go . . . into all the world, and preach the gospel to every creature." But first they must tarry until they are endued with power from on high. The Spirit-

filled life is no luxury; it is a "must" for all who would be His obedient followers.

He who issued this command had himself been clothed with the Spirit before He entered upon His ministry among men. In one of his sermons Simon Peter reminded his hearers "how God anointed Jesus of Nazareth with the Holy Ghost and with power" (Acts 10:38*a*). At the dawn of His ministry Jesus read one Sabbath from the scroll of Isaiah, "The Spirit of the Lord is upon me, because he hath anointed me to preach the gospel to the poor . . ." Then He announced to His friends of Nazareth, "This day is this scripture fulfilled in your ears" (Luke 4:18, 21). He who received the Spirit without measure wills to baptize His followers with the Holy Spirit.

To these last commands of Jesus the first-generation Christians were obedient. We can but imagine the heightened expectancy, mingled perhaps with some questioning, as the days stretched beyond a week. Seven, eight, nine—ten days they waited. "And when the day of Pentecost was fully come," it *suddenly* happened—"they were all filled with the Holy Ghost." These followers of Jesus had been called, converted, and kept by Christ (John 17:6-16). Following His death and resurrection He had appeared to them and opened the Scriptures to their understanding. Their hearts burned within them as He communed with them (Luke 24:13-32). He breathed upon them during those forty days an initial measure of the Spirit (John 20:22). Although these disciples were crossing the line of dispensations, there is unmistakable evidence that before Pentecost they were brought up to the full level of the regenerated experience. Yet they were locked behind closed doors "for fear of the Jews." They were not inwardly released because they were not yet *fully possessed* of God. Nor are *we* equipped to stand the pressures of living for Christ and of witnessing for Him in an unfriendly environment without the baptism with the Holy Spirit. *We* stand in need of the Spirit's fullness if we are to be effective Christians. How shall we receive it? *Utter obedience.* Said Peter, "And we are his witnesses of these things; and so is also the Holy Ghost, whom God hath given to them that *obey* him" (Acts 5:32). Who could estimate what would happen if all Christ's disciples should obey His command to be filled with the Spirit?

2. *The Continued Obedience of the Early Church.* The secret of the success of the Church in Acts is not hard to find. The apostles held true to Christ's command. They were restless until their converts had been filled with the Spirit. They preached repentance and proclaimed to their generation that Jesus was the promised Messiah. Yet they knew that forgiveness was not the end, but the gateway to a Spirit-filled life. Their ministry of preaching repentance and faith was but a means to an end—the spiritual restoration in holiness of the human personality. "And so it is, as the Old Testament type portrays, God brought His people of former times out of Egypt that He might bring them into the promised land of Canaan. We too are to be brought out of the bondage of sin in order that we may be brought into the spiritual freedom and liberty of a purified heart and nature."[1]

a. The Samaritan Revival. Reading the Book of Acts we come upon the report of the evangelizing of Samaria. Philip the Evangelist was the human instrument of this first awakening outside of Jerusalem. We read that Philip "preached Christ unto them." "There was great joy in that city" as God moved in with mighty power. Then we come upon this significant paragraph: "Now when the apostles which were at Jerusalem heard

[1]H. V. Miller, *When He Is Come* (Kansas City: Nazarene Publishing House, 1941), p. 8.

that Samaria had received the word of God, they sent unto them Peter and John: who, when they were come down, prayed for them, that they might receive the Holy Ghost: (for as yet he was fallen upon none of them: only they were baptized in the name of the Lord Jesus.) Then laid they their hands on them, and they received the Holy Ghost" (Acts 8:5-17).

The dominant concern of the apostles is apparent. The moment they heard of the stirring revival which was taking place under Philip they dispatched two of their own number to climax the ministry of Philip by proclaiming the baptism with the Holy Spirit. Here is clear evidence that the apostles preached two epochal crises in Christian experience and that they understood justification as the gateway to the sanctifying and empowering presence of the Spirit in the lives of those who have believed.

b. Saul of Tarsus. In the ninth chapter of Acts we encounter the dramatic conversion of Saul as he was en route to Damascus to arrest any who might be of "this way." In a blinding light of supernatural revelation the Tarsian was mightily changed. Immediately God went into action. He deputized an unknown layman by the name of Ananias to baptize this future apostle of the gentiles. After reassurance from the Lord that the arch persecutor was genuinely converted, "Ananias went his way, and entered into the house; and putting his hands on him said, *Brother Saul,* the Lord, even Jesus, that appeared unto thee in the way as thou camest, hath sent me, that thou mightest receive thy sight, and *be filled with the Holy Ghost*" (Acts 9:17). The comment of F. F. Bruce is significant and typical: "Ananias laid his hands on Saul, but it was the power of Christ that in the same moment enlightened his eyes and filled him with the Holy Spirit."[2] The flame was spreading.

[2]*Commentary on the Book of Acts* (Grand Rapids: Eerdmans, 1955), p. 201.

c. Cornelius and Family. The pattern is becoming inrceasingly clear. Chapters ten and eleven record the case of the first outright gentile Pentecost. The subjects were the Roman centurion Cornelius and his household. The human agent was the Apostle Peter. Technically Cornelius was a God-fearer—a gentile believer in the one true God but not a circumcised proselyte to the faith of Israel. He was one of the thousands of dissatisfied gentiles of that day who had turned to the Jewish synagogue for spiritual guidance. Diligent in the three recognized religious duties of prayer, fasting, and almsdeeds, he met the rigorous test laid down by Christ for these duties—he performed them as in the eyes of God (Acts 10:1-4). Peter was impressed that here was a man and his family who, in spite of their limited light were right in the sight of God: "Then Peter opened his mouth, and said, Of a truth I perceive that God is no respecter of persons: but in every nation he that feareth him, and worketh righteousness, is *accepted with him*" (Acts 10:34-35).

The apostle had but finished the introduction of his sermon when "the Holy Ghost fell on all them which heard the word. And they of the circumcision which believed were astonished, as many as came with Peter, because that on the Gentiles also was poured out the gift of the Holy Ghost." Following this baptism with the Spirit the family were baptized with water. Rehearsing this incident later in Jerusalem, Peter said, "As I began to speak, the Holy Ghost fell on them, as on us at the beginning. Then remembered I the word of the Lord, how that he said, John indeed baptized with water; but ye shall be baptized with the Holy Ghost" (Acts 11:15-16). For the apostles, salvation was not complete until men had received the baptism with the Holy Spirit. To lead men into justification and leave them there was unthinkable. With Wesley they believed that *God justifies us in order to sanctify us.* Salvation is not fully effective until by the infilling of the Spirit the sin problem is solved (Acts 11:13-14).

d. The Ephesian Disciples. The final incident to which we should give attention is the one with which this chapter opens, recounted in the eighteenth and nineteenth chapters of Acts. At Ephesus, Paul found a dozen men whose knowledge of Christ was defective. The implication is strong that they had been converted under the eloquent Apollos from Alexandria. Apollos' knowledge of Christianity seems to have been limited to the beginnings of the gospel. He preached repentance and faith in Jesus as the Messiah, but he apparently knew nothing of Calvary and Pentecost. When the friends of Paul, Aquila and Priscilla, heard this man preach, they were impressed by his sincere zeal and his knowledge of the Old Testament prophecies of Christ; but they detected a lack. So they took him aside "and expounded unto him the way of God more perfectly" (Acts 18:24-28).

A congregation seldom rises above the spiritual life of its leader. Apollos' converts knew only the level of Christian experience they had been taught by him. It was to these believers, we have seen, that Paul put the burning question, "Have ye received the Holy Ghost since ye believed?" Or as most modern versions render it, "Did you receive the Holy Spirit when you believed?" Dr. J. B. Chapman used to say, "In either case their answer was No." Although they were true disciples of Christ, they had not received the sanctifying baptism with the Holy Spirit. They had not so much as heard that the Holy Spirit had been given. They knew nothing of the infilling and indwelling of the divine Comforter.

Many modern Christians are members of First Church, Ephesus. They betray by their walk and by their talk a woeful ignorance of the Holy Spirit. *The gift of the Spirit is the lost note in modern Christianity.* "Today's church lacks something that the New Testament church had. And that lack is somehow tied up with the Holy Spirit—so abundantly mentioned on every page of those records, so manifestly present with power in the life of that church; but so seldom even named in modern Christianity, so strange to our everyday experience." These are the words of a contemporary Protestant preacher.[3] *It is time that we strike again the New Testament note.* As Paul moved into Ephesus with instruction and prayer until that little band of Christians were baptized with the Spirit, so must the modern Church pay the price in faithful preaching and prayer until He comes in blessed fullness to sanctify and empower His people. "And when he is come, he will reprove the world of sin, and of righteousness, and of judgment" (John 16:8).

Have *you* received the Holy Spirit since *you* believed? Do you know *Him* in His intimate and precious presence within? Have your futility and failure been swallowed up in His fullness? Has He come to abide within your heart? If you know that you are His child but are conscious of this lack within, the promise is for you. "If ye love me, keep my commandments. And I will pray the Father, and he shall give you another Comforter, that he may abide with you for ever; even the Spirit of truth; whom the world cannot receive, because it seeth him not, neither knoweth him: but ye know him; for he dwelleth with you, and shall be in you" (John 14:15-17).

B. The Temple of the Spirit

The high teaching of the New Testament is that the Church made up of Spirit-filled believers is the true temple of God, "an habitation of God through the Spirit" (Eph. 2:18-22). All that the Temple in Jerusalem was —and more—the Church is. It is the place where God

[3]Albert C. Winn, "Living and Walking by the Spirit," *Interpretation,* VIII, 3, p. 315.

dwells and manifests His Shekinah glory. Writing to the Corinthian church Paul asked, "Know ye not that ye are the temple of God, and that the Spirit of God dwelleth in you?" (I Cor. 3:16) Here the collective body of the Church is declared to be the holy temple of God. When the Spirit descended at Pentecost to indwell the people of God, the Jerusalem Temple was displaced by that temple not made with hands—the Church of the living God.

1. *The Spirit-baptized Church.* On the Day of Pentecost the Holy Spirit filled His true temple. Many years before when King Solomon dedicated the house he had made for the Lord, there had been a foregleam of this outpouring: "Now when Solomon had made an end of praying, the fire came down from heaven, and consumed the burnt offering and the sacrifices; and the glory of the Lord filled the house. And the priests could not enter into the house of the Lord, because the glory of the Lord filled the Lord's house. And when all the children of Israel saw how the fire came down, and the glory of the Lord upon the house, they bowed themselves with their faces to the ground upon the pavement, and worshipped, and praised the Lord, saying, For he is good; for his mercy endureth for ever" (II Chron. 7:1-3). But at Pentecost a surpassing glory prompted the people to ask in utter amazement, "What meaneth this?" and after Peter's Pentecostal sermon to cry out from pierced hearts, "Men and brethren, what shall we do?" (Acts 2:12, 37)

"And when the day of Pentecost *was fully come,* they were all with one accord in one place. And suddenly there came a sound from heaven as of a rushing mighty wind, and it filled all the house where they were sitting. And there appeared unto them cloven tongues like as of fire, and it sat upon each of them. And they were all filled with the Holy Ghost, and began to speak with other tongues, as the Spirit gave them utterance"

(Acts 2:1-4). *Here is the New Testament pattern of the Church.* The glory and power of God must fill the Church collectively and her members individually. The sound as of the rushing mighty wind suggests that they were *all* filled with the Spirit. The cloven tongues as of fire sat upon the head of *each* of them, suggesting that the experience was personal. "Keep the glory down!" was the constant insistence of Dr. P. F. Bresee. We must ever seek "the simplicity and spiritual power manifest in the primitive New Testament Church."[4]

2. *The Spirit-filled Church.* A Spirit-baptized church from time to time experiences a renewal of the Spirit. Pentecost precipitated fierce opposition. The authorities of Jerusalem did their utmost to silence the witness of the infant Church. Peter and John were haled before the Sanhedrin and commanded to keep silent concerning the name of Jesus. But these intrepid warriors came back with these words: "Whether it be right in the sight of God to hearken unto you more than unto God, judge ye. For we cannot but speak the things which we have seen and heard" (Acts 4:19-20). Then being released, they called the Church to prayer. "And when they had prayed, the place was shaken where they were assembled together; *and they were all filled with the Holy Ghost,* and they spake the word of God with boldness. . . . and great grace was upon them all" (Acts 4:31, 33). This may have been a new Pentecost for the many who had been added to the original company of believers, but it was most certainly a time also of fresh anointing and empowering for the 120. "One baptism, many anointings"—this is the New Testament formula. Our theology must be kept elastic enough *to make for reality.* Only as we are clothed in the Spirit's courageous power and caring love can we make an impact upon the world.

[4]*Manual*, Church of the Nazarene, paragraph 23.

Only as we have that plus of God within and upon us can we melt the cold indifference of society about us. "Spirit of the living God, fall fresh on me!"

3. *The Lordship of the Spirit.* To read Acts is to discover one truth writ large: The Holy Spirit was the Executive of the Church. He it was who prompted, who spoke, who constrained, who guided. The New Testament Church was the vehicle of the Spirit. If we are to discover the simplicity and power of New Testament Christianity, we must honor and obey the Spirit. Let us turn to the records.

The church at Antioch is at prayer. We read: "As they ministered to the Lord, and fasted, the Holy Ghost said, Separate me Barnabas and Saul for the work whereunto I have called them. So they, being sent forth by the *Holy Ghost,* departed" (Acts 13:2, 4). This was the inauguration of the gentile mission of the Church. World evangelism is not the scheme of churchmen seeking to enlarge an institution; it is the strategy of the Spirit of God. The story of missions down through the centuries is the story of the Spirit's constant stirring of the Church to reach out. He will not let the Church settle down and die; again and again He finds new instruments of His purposes. He is the Spirit of missions, and He has His own program of world evangelism.

With converted gentiles in their membership the Church faced a new problem. The Pharisaical element in the Jerusalem congregation objected vigorously to the practice of Paul and Barnabas in receiving uncircumcised converts into the fold, "saying, That it was needful to circumcise them, and to command them to keep the law of Moses" (Acts 15:5). A general assembly of the Church was called to settle this question. After hearing the witnesses and reviewing the case, the apostles drew up a letter for circulation in the disturbed areas of the Church: "For it seemed good to the *Holy Ghost,* and to us, to lay upon you no greater burden than these necessary things" (Acts 15:28). So conscious were these leaders of being possessed and controlled by the Holy Spirit that He was given prior mention as the chief Author of their decision. He is the Author of unity and peace in the body of Christ for the sake of maximum effectiveness in reaching a lost world.

The apostles, moreover, were conscious of the Spirit's direction as they chose pastors of local congregations. Luke informs us that human leaders ordained elders in every church (Acts 14:23). But to the elders of Ephesus, Paul could say, "Take heed . . . to all the flock, over which the *Holy Ghost* hath made you overseers" (Acts 20:28).

The Spirit also administered the judgments of God within the churches. When Ananias and Sapphira entered into an unholy compact to deceive God's people, Ananias was confronted by Simon Peter. "Why hath Satan filled thine heart to lie to the *Holy Ghost?"* Peter solemnly asked. Then when Sapphira revealed her part in the plot, Peter queried, "How is it that ye have agreed together to tempt the Spirit of the Lord?" (Acts 5:3, 9) The couple had been detected in a plan to see how far they could go in presuming upon the forbearance of the Spirit of God; and they had gone too far. We must honor and obey the Spirit as the Lord of the Church.

We would do well to ponder this truth. The Holy Spirit is the Executive of the Godhead. In planning and carrying out the work of the Church we must seek His mind by waiting before Him in prayer and openness. We must put aside all personal considerations from our thinking and ask only that His will be done. In our teaching and preaching we must give the Spirit His rightful place as Lord of His holy temple.

4. *The Guidance of the Spirit.* "As many as are led by the Spirit of God, they are the sons of God" (Rom.

8:14). Acts offers abundant evidence that the Spirit is graciously present to guide *individual* Christians. After breaking with Barnabas over the advisability of taking along John Mark on their second journey, Paul formed a new missionary party. He chose Silas as his new partner, and at Lystra, Timothy joined the party. This trio set out for the Roman province of Asia in Asia Minor. But wait! They "were forbidden of the *Holy Ghost* to preach the word in Asia." "Then, after they were come to Mysia, they assayed to go into Bithynia: but the *Spirit* suffered them not" (Acts 16:6-7). This little missionary band found themselves hemmed in on every side by the Spirit of God, who was hurrying them on to Troas. Here Luke was waiting and Paul was to receive the Macedonian call which was to plant the Church for the first time on European soil. Whether this overruling guidance was through the Inner Voice or from the lips of Spirit-inspired prophets is incidental. In either case these preachers were not carrying out their own preconceived plans—they were following the leadings of the Spirit of God. Sometimes God guides through the check of the Spirit; at other times He directs us through other Christians who become the instruments of the Spirit for us. "God leads His dear children along."

Furthermore, in times of testing when they were called to witness before their enemies, the disciples found that the promise Jesus had left them was true. While yet with them He had said, "But when they deliver you up, take no thought how or what ye shall speak: for it shall be given you in the same hour what ye shall speak. For it is not ye that speak, but the Spirit of your Father which speaketh in you" (Matt. 10:19-20). And so it was. When the authorities questioned Peter concerning the power by which he had healed the lame man at the Gate Beautiful, we are told that Peter answered them, being "filled with the Holy Ghost" (Acts 4:8). Paul found the same wonderful help from the Spirit on Cyprus when he was withstood by the sorcerer Elymas (Acts 13:9). If we keep ourselves fully yielded to the leading of the Holy Spirit and entirely devoted to God's purposes, we can count on His help when needed.

Summary. Acts gives us a picture of the Church as the temple of the Spirit. God wills and yearns to fill His Church with His power and glory. Within the Church the Holy Spirit is the Executive of the Godhead. The entire life of the Church must be subject to His leadership as we wait before Him in prayer and fasting and as we sincerely seek His perfect will. The guidance of the Spirit, however, is not given to the Church collectively except as it is first given to individuals. We must live personally under His sovereign sway. The Spirit's guidance comes not only from within but sometimes from other Christians who know both His mind and us objectively.

Questions for Discussion

1. What justification can you make for the claim that the Book of Acts might be called *The Acts of the Holy Spirit?*

2. Why is the baptism with the Holy Spirit a "must" for Christians?

3. Discuss the statement, "God justifies us in order that He might sanctify us." Support your answer from the Book of Acts.

4. What can we do to help insure a continued emphasis on the necessity of the baptism with the Holy Spirit and Christian holiness in our church?

5. What do we mean by saying the Holy Spirit is "the Executive of the Godhead" within the Church?

6. How does the Spirit guide us today?

III

The Age of the Spirit

But this is that which was spoken by the prophet Joel; And it shall come to pass in the last days, saith God, I will pour out of my Spirit upon all flesh (Acts 2:16-17).

When tourists visited Los Angeles at the turn of the century, they were taken by the old frame building which housed the congregation of the First Church of the Nazarene. Such divine glory rested upon that noble band of Nazarenes that their humble house of worship came to be known affectionately as the "glory barn."

Concerning that edifice Dr. Phineas F. Bresee wrote: "It was the fire that burned within that guilded its boards with glory and made them shimmer and shine with the light of heaven. When the multitude is gathered, and there are hundreds of one mind and heart, and the Holy Ghost descends in His plenitude and power, that place is garnished with a beauty and glory in comparison with which all the adornings of Solomon's temple would be barrenness. Every board shines with the jewelled beauty of the New Jerusalem. What are carved marble and over-laying of gold and trimmings of silver; what are arches and turrets and spires, in comparison with the beauty of the Lord and the glory of the Divine Presence?"

It was Pentecost which ushered in the day of the Spirit, making possible such a glorious manifestation of God in the midst of His Church. But Pentecost cannot be properly appreciated apart from its background. Pentecost was the fulfillment of the deepest and broadest stream of Old Testament prophecy. The coming of Christ was simply the preparatory stage for the universal outpouring of the Spirit. The Old Testament foresees the Messianic age as preeminently the age of the Spirit.

To understand the significance of Pentecost, therefore, we must view it within the framework of the Old Testament and appreciate it as the fulfillment of Moses' wistful longing when he cried, "Would God that all the Lord's people were prophets, and that the Lord would put his spirit upon them!" (Num. 11:29)

A. The Holy Spirit in the Old Testament

There are altogether eighty-six references to the Spirit of God in the Old Testament. Fourteen of these are to be found in the first five books of Moses, although Leviticus has no reference and Deuteronomy only one. Thirteen references appear in Isaiah and fifteen in Ezekiel. Judges and I and II Samuel contain fourteen references between them, with Psalms having six. The remaining sixteen references are scattered through the other eleven books of the Old Testament. Most of the action of the Spirit is expressed by the term "Spirit of God," with only three references to "the Holy Spirit."

For our purposes we may divide all these passages into three groups: (1) those which have to do with the Spirit's relation to the world in general; (2) those which have to do with redemption; (3) those referring to the Messiah and the age of the Spirit.

1. *The Spirit's Relation to the World in General.* The Holy Spirit is associated with creation: "The spirit of God moved upon the face of the waters" (Gen. 1:2). He is associated with human life in general. Job said, "The spirit of God is in my nostrils" (Job 27:3). Speaking to the men who lived before the Flood, the Lord said, "My spirit shall not always strive with man" (Gen. 6:3). The Spirit bestows supernatural wisdom: "And Pharaoh said unto his servants, Can we find such a one as this is, a man in whom the spirit of God is?"

(Gen. 41:38) He is associated with intellectual and artistic capacity: "And Moses said unto the children of Israel, See, the Lord hath called by name Bezaleel . . . and he hath filled him with the spirit of God, in wisdom, in understanding, and in knowledge, and in all manner of workmanship" (Exod. 35:30-31). The Spirit is God everywhere present in His universe: "Whither shall I go from thy spirit? or whither shall I flee from thy presence? If I ascend up into heaven, thou art there: if I make my bed in hell, behold, thou art there. If I take the wings of the morning, and dwell in the uttermost parts of the sea; even there shall thy hand lead me, and thy right hand shall hold me" (Ps. 139:7-10). He is personal Spirit, permeating yet distinct from His creation. He is present, moreover, not only as the sustaining power of the world, but also as a disturbing moral influence in the lives of sinful men. The Spirit of God *is* the Holy Spirit.

These passages show that the Old Testament takes into account the general relations of the Spirit to the world; but in order to understand the Christian teaching of the Holy Spirit we must examine rather carefully those passages which have to do with the Spirit's relation to God's redemptive purposes for men.

2. *The Spirit's Relation to God's Redemptive Purposes.* The word translated "spirit" in the Old Testament meant originally "wind" or "breath." It suggests a desert wind suddenly whipped up to fury and makes us think of the power of a tornado. Sometimes it is used to refer to the "breath" of a man's nostrils when he is extremely excited. The word came thus to mean *supernatural power which laid hold upon a person,* reinforcing him to do a divinely appointed task.

In Judges we read how "the spirit of the Lord came upon" Othniel, Gideon, Jephthah, and Samson, empowering them to champion the cause of Israel against its enemies (Judg. 3:10; 6:34; 11:29; 13:25). In I Samuel we read an interesting account of Saul of Kish. To Saul Samuel says, "And the spirit of the Lord will come upon thee, and thou shalt prophesy unto them, and shalt be turned into another man. And it was so, that when he had turned his back to go from Samuel, God gave him another heart . . . and the spirit of God came upon him, and he prophesied" (I Sam. 10:6, 9-10).

Later on the Spirit is the Author of prophetic inspiration to the writing prophets. Ezekiel testifies: "And he said unto me, Son of man, stand upon thy feet, and I will speak unto thee. And the spirit entered into me when he spake unto me, and set me upon my feet, that I heard him that spake unto me. And he said unto me . . ." (Ezek. 2:1-3). In the following chapter we read, "I heard also the noise . . . of a great rushing. So the spirit lifted me up, and took me away, and I went in bitterness, in the heat of my spirit; but the hand of the Lord was strong upon me" (Ezek. 3:13-14; cf. Acts 2:2).

The prevailing idea in all these passages is not that of making men righteous or holy, but of endowing them in times of national crisis or for the purpose of divine revelation. Two points are worth remembering: (1) The coming of the Spirit upon individuals in the Old Testament was a transient experience. There is no hint that the Holy Spirit came as a permanent Indweller; rather, He "came mightily upon them" for prophecy or for some immediate task. (2) To put the same idea in a different way, He did not come to sanctify the souls of men. John said specifically, "The Holy Ghost was not yet given" (John 7:39).

Three references to the "holy spirit" seem to suggest the New Testament meaning. In his brokenhearted penitence David prayed, "Cast me not away from thy presence; and take not thy *holy spirit* from me" (Ps. 51:11). "Thy holy spirit" here is exactly parallel with "thy presence." Yet the idea of sanctity is there too. The other two references are in a single passage. "But they rebelled, and grieved his *holy Spirit*: therefore he was turned to be their enemy, and himself fought against them. Then he remembered the days of old, Moses, and his people, saying, Where is he that brought them up out of the sea with the shepherds of his flock? where is he that put his holy Spirit in the midst of them?" (Isa. 63:10-11, ASV) The *Holy Spirit* here is the presence of God, the Holy One, in their midst. But even these passages fall far short of the New Testament doctrine of the Holy Spirit.

3. *Prophecies of the Messiah and the Age of the Spirit.* By far the most important passages which deal with the Holy Spirit are those which are predictive of the Messiah and of Pentecost.

a. Prophecies of the Messiah. "In contrast to the heroes, kings, and prophets of the past, upon whom the Spirit came only as an occasional and temporary visitant, the promised shoot of the stem of Jesse is one upon whom the Spirit of the Lord will *remain*."[1] "And the spirit of the Lord," says Isaiah, "shall *rest upon* him, the spirit of wisdom and understanding, the spirit of counsel and might, the spirit of knowledge and of the fear of the Lord" (Isa. 11:2). Again the Lord says: "Behold my servant, whom I uphold; mine elect, in whom my soul delighteth; *I have put my spirit upon him*: he shall bring forth judgment to the Gentiles. . . . He shall not fail nor be discouraged, till he have set judgment in the earth: and the isles shall wait for his law" (Isa. 42:1-4). The Messiah was to be the Anointed of the Lord, the Recipient and Bearer of the Spirit.

b. Prophecies of Pentecost. The expectation of the Messiah, upon whom the Spirit should come to rest and abide, was only part of the hope of the people of God.

[1]George S. Hendry, *The Holy Spirit in Christian Theology* (Philedelphia: Westminster Press, 1956), p. 17.

The vision of the Messiah or Servant of the Lord leads on to the expectation of an outpouring of the Spirit on the whole of God's people and ultimately upon all flesh.

In Isaiah we read:

> *I will pour water upon him that is thirsty, and floods upon the dry ground: I will pour my spirit upon thy seed, and my blessing upon thine offspring* (Isa. 44:3).

In Ezekiel the Lord promises:

> *Then will I sprinkle clean water upon you, and ye shall be clean: from all your filthiness and from all your idols, will I cleanse you. A new heart also will I give you, and a new spirit will I put within you: and I will take away the stony heart out of your flesh, and I will give you an heart of flesh. And I will put my spirit within you, and cause you to walk in my statutes, and ye shall keep my judgments, and do them* (Ezek. 36:25-27).

In Malachi we have this certain word:

> *Behold, I will send my messenger, and he shall prepare the way before me: and the Lord, whom ye seek, shall suddenly come to his temple . . . But who may abide the day of his coming? and who shall stand when he appeareth? for he is like a refiner's fire, and like fullers' soap . . . and he shall purify the sons of Levi, and purge them as gold and silver, that they may offer unto the Lord an offering in righteousness* (Mal. 3:1-3).

The universal prophecy is found in Joel:

> *And it shall come to pass afterward, that I will pour out my spirit upon all flesh; and your sons and your daughters shall prophesy, your old men shall dream dreams, your young men shall see visions: and also upon the servants and upon the handmaids in those days will I pour out my spirit* (Joel 2:28-29).

Although the Spirit is not expressly mentioned in the passage, Jeremiah's prophecy of the new covenant (31:31-34) should not here be overlooked.

An understanding of these prophecies is absolutely essential to our grasping the significance of the Messiah and His ministry. The Messianic age was to be marked by a *universal* and *sanctifying* outpouring of the Spirit—first on Israel and then on all flesh. God was going to put His Holy Spirit *within* the hearts of His people, enabling them to do His holy and righteous will. This came to be the clear hope of the Jews in the period preceding the New Testament. They believed that, because of the sins of the nation, the Spirit had ascended to heaven about the time of Malachi, but that He would return at the time of the Messiah to be diffused upon all people, both Jews and gentiles. The prophecies we have just quoted provided the basis for this hope—*that in the day of the Messiah there would be an unprecedented gift of the Holy Spirit, not only removing their guilt but also sanctifying their inner nature.* Among the rabbis Simeon b. Johai gave this typical paraphrase of Ezek. 36:26: "And God said, 'In this age, because the evil impulse exists in you, ye have sinned against me; but in the age to come I will *eradicate* it from you.' "

In the light of this expectancy the dramatic predictions of John the Baptist are illuminated. The last of the Old Testament prophets, John, gathers all the rays of Messianic hope into focus when he announces: "I indeed baptize you with water unto repentance: but he that cometh after me is mightier than I, whose shoes I am not worthy to bear: he shall baptize you with the Holy Ghost, and with fire: whose fan is in his hand, and he will throughly purge his floor, and gather his wheat into the garner; but he will burn up the chaff with unquenchable fire" (Matt. 3:11-12). The kingdom of God is at hand!

B. The Holy Spirit in the New Testament

The Old Testament has given us the setting within which to understand the role of Christ and the gift of the Spirit at Pentecost. The New Testament emphasis is obvious: Christ has ushered in the long-expected day of the Spirit.

1. *The Holy Spirit in the Gospels.* In the first three Gospels there are a number of references to the Holy Spirit. Matthew has twelve, none of them related to the person of Christ. Mark has six, all quoted by Matthew. Luke contains eighteen references to the Holy Spirit, eight of them explaining the Spirit's relationship to Jesus as the Christ.

a. The Holy Spirit and the Birth of Jesus. We shall consider these specific references in the order of their importance.

(1) Luke tells us that Zacharias and Elisabeth, the parents of John the Baptist, were filled with the Holy Spirit. "Elisabeth was filled with the Holy Ghost" and pronounced a blessing upon the Virgin Mary (Luke 1:41-45), while Zacharias prophesied under the Spirit's inspiration (Luke 1:68-69). The Holy Spirit also came upon the aged Simeon in the Temple when he recognized the infant Saviour (Luke 2:22-32). Here we have something like the gift of the Spirit for prophecy in the Old Testament, a temporary infilling of the Spirit.

(2) Of John the Baptist, however, it is said that he was "filled with the Holy Ghost, even from his mother's womb" (Luke 1:15), and that he "grew, and waxed strong in spirit" (Luke 1:80). Whatever this implies, it means that his life was in a special way under the control of God from the beginning, that he was dedicated to the Lord before he was born, and through a life of personal devotion grew to be strong in the Spirit of God. As the forerunner of Christ he stood greater than any before him. Yet Jesus said that he who is least in His kingdom is greater than John.

(3) The most precious of the Gospel passages concerning the Holy Spirit refer to Jesus' supernatural con-

ception. "And the angel answered and said unto her, The Holy Ghost shall come upon thee, and the power of the Highest shall overshadow thee: therefore also that holy thing which shall be born of thee shall be called the Son of God" (Luke 1:35; cf. Matt. 1:18-23). It was altogether fitting that the sinless Son of God should be so conceived. He was not the product of human history—He is the eternal Word made flesh.

Of us all it must be said, "That which is born of the flesh is flesh." Therefore we must be born again—of the Spirit. *But not Jesus.* His only birth was of the Spirit; His entire life from the moment of His conception was under the sanctifying control of the Holy Spirit.

b. The Holy Spirit and the Baptism of Jesus. At Jesus' baptism the Holy Spirit descended upon Him "in a bodily shape" (Luke 3:22). The Spirit did not descend upon Jesus at that precise moment, not having been upon Him before; but it was then revealed that Jesus was the permanent Bearer of the Holy Spirit. Jesus, that is, did not *become* the Messiah at His baptism. The descending dove and the voice from heaven simply *identified* Him as the Anointed of the Lord.

Furthermore, at His baptism Jesus was identified as the *Baptizer* with the Holy Spirit. "And John bare record, saying, I saw the Spirit descending from heaven like a dove, and it abode upon him. And I knew him not: but he that sent me to baptize with water, the same said unto me, *Upon whom thou shalt see the Spirit descending, and remaining on him, the same is he which baptizeth with the Holy Ghost*" (John 1:32-33).

Thus in Jesus Christ the two strains of Messianic prophecy converge. At His baptism He is disclosed as (1) the permanent Bearer of the Holy Spirit and (2) as the Baptizer with the Holy Spirit. This explains John's dramatic announcement. "The kingdom of God is at hand." The final day of the Spirit was dawning!

c. *The Holy Spirit and Jesus' Life and Ministry.* Other Gospel passages tell us how the Spirit was present with Jesus in His temptation, His preaching, His casting out of demons. His whole life in fact was a manifestation of the Holy Spirit. "The fruits of the Spirit are the virtues of Christ." *He was the perfect Pattern of the Spirit-filled life.* No speaker in tongues was He, or super-righteous bigot! So possessed of God, and yet so sane! So holy, and yet so humble! The Spirit whispers to us, "Let this mind be in you, which was also in Christ Jesus."

In one place Jesus warns against the danger of blaspheming the Holy Spirit (Matt. 12:22-32). By our willfulness we may become so spiritually blind as to attribute to Satan the works of the Spirit of God. This is a very dangerous sin because it is the destruction of that within us to which the Spirit may appeal.

Most of Jesus' specific teaching concerning the Holy Spirit came toward the close of His ministry. He was chiefly concerned to show the power of the Holy Spirit for righteous living and effective witnessing and thus to set the pattern for Pentecost. Jesus promised His disciples the Holy Spirit would give them the words to speak when they were called before authorities for His sake (Matt. 10:19-20).

The third strain of teaching concerning the Spirit has to do with the promised gift of the Spirit at Pentecost. We shall have occasion to consider these teachings carefully in later chapters; hence two promises are sufficient here to illustrate this emphasis. "Nevertheless I tell you the truth; It is expedient for you that I go away: for if I go not away, the Comforter will not come unto you; but if I depart, I will send him unto you" (John 16:7). All His promises climax in that given just prior to His ascension: "Ye shall be baptized with the Holy Ghost not many days hence" (Acts 1:5). Everything was pointing toward Pentecost.

2. *The Holy Spirit and Pentecost.* In Simon Peter's Pentecostal sermon we come upon words of tremendous import: "THIS IS THAT WHICH WAS SPOKEN BY THE PROPHET JOEL." With the announcement of Jesus' Messiahship at His baptism, the first strain of Messianic prophecy was fulfilled. Peter's proclamation at Pentecost was an announcement that the second strain was now fulfilled. If the day of the Spirit was dawning at Jesus' baptism, at Pentecost "the Sun of righteousness" had risen "with healing in his wings."

Mark well the claim of the apostle: "But this is that which was spoken by the prophet Joel; And it shall come to pass in the last days, saith God, I will pour out of my Spirit upon all flesh: and your sons and your daughters shall prophesy, and your young men shall see visions, and your old men shall dream dreams: and on my servants and on my handmaidens I will pour out in those days of my Spirit; and they shall prophesy" (Acts 2: 16-18). The days of the Messiah—forseen by the prophets—were finally here in all their glory! The "last days" of which Peter spoke began with Christ's first advent and will be consummated by the Second Coming, "that great and notable day of the Lord" (Acts 2:19-20). *Between these two events stretches the age-long day of the Spirit.* "This is the dispensation in which Jesus Christ baptizes believers with the Holy Ghost and with fire."

Pricked in their hearts by Peter's Pentecostal sermon, his hearers cried out, "Men and brethren, what shall we do? Then Peter said unto them, Repent, and be baptized every one of you in the name of Jesus Christ for the remission of sins, and ye shall receive the gift of the Holy Ghost. For the promise is unto you, and to your children, and to all that are afar off, even as many as the Lord our God shall call" (Acts 2:37-39).

What is the "promise" to which Peter refers? Plainly it is the promise of "the gift of the Holy Ghost." It is the promise of the baptism with the Holy Spirit. On

Mount Olivet our Lord "commanded them that they should not depart from Jerusalem, but wait for *the promise* of the Father, which, saith he, ye have heard of me. For John truly baptized with water; but ye shall be baptized with the Holy Ghost not many days hence" (Acts 1:4-5). The glorious promise which extends throughout this age is that we may be baptized with the Holy Spirit (cf. Acts 2:33).

The promise of the Father is "to all that are afar off." That takes us in, for we are the gentiles who were "once far off, but are now made nigh in the blood of Christ" (Eph. 2:13, ASV). But lest there be any doubt about it, Peter adds, "even as many as the Lord our God shall call." Can words be plainer? The baptism with the Holy Spirit is the birthright of every child of God throughout this age.

"This, then, is the constant emphasis of the New Testament—the work, the presence, the purity, the power of the Holy Spirit. Dispensationally all was to climax in Him. His coming to the individual heart of the believer in purifying, empowering presence was the final fruition of all the ages past. Not that He should receive the preeminence but that He might give it. It was to become His task to crystallize and conserve the work of Calvary. . . . We live today in the dispensation of the Holy Spirit. He is the sovereignly chosen member of the Trinity to carry out the purposes of God in the earth. His indwelling presence must be recognized and established as an experiential reality in the heart of everyone who would do the will of God."[2]

A Hindu with New Testament in hand confronted a missionary with this question: "Sir, I read in the New Testament Book of Acts that the disciples of Jesus received a mighty baptism with the Holy Spirit. My question to you is this, Sir, have you received this baptism?"

[2]Miller, *op. cit.*, p. 10.

Although he was university-trained, he dropped his head in confession that he was ignorant of this baptism. But he was honest. He went back to his mission and entered upon a season of prayerful seeking. He emerged a Spirit-baptized missionary and left a monument to his work in India when after many years he went to be with Jesus. What would *your* answer be to the question, "Sir, have *you* received this baptism?"

Questions for Discussion

1. What are the three groups of Old Testament passages which have to do with the Holy Spirit?

2. What can you say of the relation of the Spirit of God to the world in general?

3. How did the Spirit act upon men in Old Testament times?

4. Wherein did the work of the Holy Spirit in the Old Testament fall short of the New Testament ministry of the Spirit?

5. What did the prophecies say would be the relation of the Spirit to the Messiah?

6. What was predicted to be distinctive mark of the Messianic age?

7. What may we learn from Jesus as the pattern of Pentecost?

8. Show by the word of God that we are living in the continuing day of the Spirit.

IV

The Person of the Spirit

If ye love me, keep my commandments. And I will pray the Father, and he shall give you another Comforter, that he may abide with you for ever; even the Spirit of truth; whom the world cannot receive, because it seeth him not, neither knoweth him: but ye know him; for he dwelleth with you, and shall be in you. I will not leave you comfortless: I will come to you (John 14:15-18).

What has the Bible to say about the Holy Spirit as a Person? We cannot rightly understand His work or come into right relationship with the Holy Spirit himself, and thus know His gracious work in our souls, unless we acknowledge His true personality.

It is important that we especially emphasize the personality of the Holy Spirit:

(1) In the full Christian revelation of God, the Holy Spirit is disclosed as genuinely personal. To speak of the Holy Spirit as *it*—as an impersonal influence or power from God—is to discredit, or at least to disregard, the clear teachings of the New Testament.

(2) To think of the Holy Spirit as simply a power from God is to fall into a form of idolatry; it is to ask, "How can I get the Holy Spirit and use it?" God would thus be a power to be selfishly manipulated. If I think of the Holy Spirit as an impersonal force, I will ask, "How can I have more power?" But if I acknowledge Him as a Person, my concern will be, "How can the Holy Spirit get more of me?" Bible religion is God-centered. Such God-centeredness is guarded by faith in the Holy Spirit as the Third Person of the holy Trinity.

(3) To think of the Holy Spirit as an impersonal influence is to rob Him of the worship which is due Him as the Third Person of the adorable Trinity.

Praise God from whom all blessings flow;
Praise Him, all creatures here below;
Praise Him above, ye heav'nly host;
Praise Father, Son, and Holy Ghost.

To know and worship the Holy Spirit, however, is more than a matter of correct theology. He must come in His personal indwelling if we are to have an *inner* and *sanctifying* knowledge of Him. The passage which prefaces this chapter (John 14:15-18) became the channel of this personal knowledge to the writer. Painfully he had become aware that his life was not bearing the fruit of the Spirit. Inner unrest and occasional defeat marred his fellowship with God. His heart was yearning for the fullness of the Spirit as he was reading these sacred words. Then suddenly it happened! His heart began to burn within him as he *knew* with that knowledge which passes intellectual understanding that the Holy Spirit himself had come to abide. With the coming of the Comforter the truth suddenly became unutterably personal. For years he had believed intellectually in the personality of the Holy Spirit, but in that moment he knew Him in His personal fullness.

Glory be to the Father,
And to the Son,
And to the Holy Ghost;
As it was in the beginning,
Is now, and ever shall be,
World without end. Amen.

A. The Personality of the Holy Spirit

When we speak of the Holy Spirit as a Person we do not mean that He is a bodily creature. Human persons as we know them in this life have bodies, but a body is only a means for expressing true personality. A person thinks, feels, acts. A person also makes moral choices.

1. *Personal Qualities Belonging to the Holy Spirit.*

a. Intelligence. When we affirm that the Spirit is intelligent, then we are affirming His personality. The prophet Isaiah asks: "Who hath directed the spirit of the Lord, or being his counsellor hath taught him? With whom took he counsel, and who instructed him, and taught him in the path of judgment, and taught him knowledge, and shewed to him the way of understanding?" (Isa. 40:13-14) The same truth meets us in the New Testament: "For what man knoweth the things of a man, save the spirit of man which is in him? even so the things of God knoweth no man, but the Spirit of God. For who hath known the mind of the Lord, that he may instruct him?" (I Cor. 2:11, 16) In Rom. 8:26-27, Paul speaks of the *mind* of the Spirit, suggesting that there is a meaning in our prayer beyond that of which we are aware. The true intent of real prayer is the result of the work of the Holy Spirit, who guides us as we pray.

b. Feeling. The Holy Spirit has personal feelings and emotions. In Rom. 15:30 we read: "Now I beseech you, brethren, for the Lord Jesus Christ's sake, and for the *love* of the Spirit, that ye strive together with me in your prayers to God for me." In Eph. 4:30 we are warned: "Grieve not the holy Spirit of God." The Holy Spirit within creates divine love in our hearts, but if we give way to an unchristlike spirit He is grieved. To persist in a wrong attitude is to grieve Him away and break His seal.

c. Decision and Purpose. In Corinthians, Paul discusses spiritual gifts. They are varied, he says, to serve different functions within the body of Christ. "But all these worketh that one and the selfsame Spirit, dividing to every man severally *as he will*" (I Cor. 12:11). A person's gift is not according to his own will or choice but according to the choice of the Spirit. Although God probably takes into account our natural abilities, in the final analysis the Spirit's gifts are supernatural bestowments made according to the Spirit's will. Here we confront the matter of the call of the Spirit. I may prefer to follow a certain line of work, but I feel inwardly impelled to another type of service. The call of the old prophets and the call today to the ministry or the mission field are evidence of the planning of the Spirit. The Spirit is not a divine power we use according to our will; He is a Divine Person who wants to use us according to His will.

d. Moral Choices. The title "Holy" applied to the Spirit of God indicates that He is a moral Personality. Holiness in the moral sense can apply only to a personal being. The same conclusion concerning His moral nature is implied by the fact that He is a Member of the Trinity. He who is called the Spirit of God and the Spirit of Christ must be the Holy Spirit. In the awesome warning Jesus gave to the Pharisees against blaspheming the Spirit, "their danger was the danger of disregarding or defying the ultimate moral power of the universe, of doing this in such a way as to destroy all power of moral discrimination in themselves."[1] Moreover, when the Spirit convicts us, He convicts of *sin* and of *righteousness,* and when He enters our hearts in regenerating and sanctifying power He transforms us morally. It is because He is a moral Person that He is grieved by sin.

2. *Personal Acts Belonging to the Holy Spirit.* Even a casual reading of the New Testament convices us that the Spirit *acts* as a Person. Jesus promised His disciples that the Spirit would teach them all things and *bring to*

[1]W. T. Conner, *The Work of the Holy Spirit* (Nashville: Broadman Press, 1949), p. 179.

remembrance all that He had said unto them while with them in the flesh (John 14:26). Notice the verbs in this passage: "Howbeit when he, the Spirit of truth, is come, he will *guide* you into all truth: for he shall not *speak* of himself; but whatsoever he shall *hear,* that shall he speak: and he will *shew* you things to come. He shall *glorify* me: for he shall *receive* of mine, and shall shew it unto you" (John 16:13-14). In Acts the Spirit is said to speak, to send, to forbid, and to counsel.

3. *Personal Pronouns Employed in Reference to the Spirit.* The Greek word translated "Spirit" in the New Testament is neuter in gender. As the Hebrew word translated "Spirit," it also means "wind" or "breath" in its original usage. But in the Upper Room discourses in John's Gospel (John 14:17, 26, *et al.*) the laws of Greek grammar are defied. Personal pronouns are employed although the Greek would dictate the neuter. We do read in a few places the phrase "the Spirit itself" in the King James Version (Rom. 8:16, 26). In these cases the Spirit's personality is not being denied, for the work ascribed to Him in each instance is personal. The writer was simply following the requirements of correct grammatical usage. The American and Revised Standard versions render these phrases "the Spirit *himself.*"

4. *The Spirit Associated with the Father and the Son.* The New Testament parallels the Holy Spirit with the other Persons of the Godhead. The Great Commission commands us to baptize "in the name of the Father, and of the Son, and of the Holy Ghost" (Matt. 28:19). Paul's moving benediction in II Corinthians reads: "The grace of the Lord Jesus Christ, and the love of God, and the communion of the Holy Ghost, be with you all" (13:14).

The New Testament equates the Spirit with God. After accusing Ananias of lying to the Holy Spirit, Peter charged, "Thou hast not lied unto men, but unto God."

If the Spirit is God, and God is personal, then the Spirit is personal.

B. The Trinity

Our consideration of the personality of the Holy Spirit has introduced us to the doctrine of the Trinity. Intelligent, effective Christians must have some understanding of this admittedly difficult doctrine. We cannot expect to fully comprehend the mystery of the Infinite. If we could, God would not be God. Mystery should inspire awe, worship, adoration. But mystery must not involve us in contradiction. The doctrine of the Trinity may be *beyond* reason; it must not be so stated as to be unreasonable.

1. *There Is One God.* The entire Bible is monotheistic, the disclosure of the one true and living God. The Old Testament Shema summarizes the faith of both the Jew and the Christian: "Hear, O Israel: The Lord our God is one Lord: and thou shalt love the Lord thy God with all thine heart, and with all thy soul, and with all thy might" (Deut. 6:4-5). Jesus said, "Think not that I am come to destroy the law, or the prophets: I am not come to destroy, but to fulfil" (Matt. 5:17). Jesus did not come to set aside, but to fulfill the monotheistic faith of Judaism. The New Testament must not be interpreted so as to make three Gods. Paul says flatly, "There is *one God.*" There is only one Divine Being. Reason supports this claim of revelation. Science knows that we are living in a *universe,* a unified system of order and intelligence presided over and sustained by Supreme Intelligence. The ultimate principle of the universe is One. This is so evident to reason that the old philosophers of Greece came to a belief in one God apart from the special revelation of the Bible.

2. *There Are Three "Persons" in the One God.* The Bible teaches—by clear intimation in the Old Testa-

ment and by explicit statement in the New Testament—that the unity of God is not a rigid, mathematical unity. It is a rich complexity.

God is one; God is three. But God is not three in the same way that He is one—that would be nonsense. *He is one Divine Being within whom there are three centers of personal consciousness.* The Early Church said that God is one substance, within which there are three Persons. But the word "substance" suggests material stuff to the average person—*and God is Spirit.* Being is a better word than substance. Though we cannot comprehend God, this much we know: He is not *solitary,* He is *social.*

Glory to God in Trinity,
Whose names have mysteries unknown:
In essence one, in Persons three;
A social nature, yet alone.

—Isaac Watts

a. New Testament Teaching. The New Testament clearly teaches that the Father is God, the Son is God, the Holy Spirit is God; and further, that wherever and whenever we meet one Person of the Godhead we meet *God.* The Father is God, Christ is God, the Spirit is God.

Dr. Samuel Chadwick observes: "As it pleased God that in His Son should dwell the fullness of the godhead bodily, so it has pleased Him that in the dispensation of the Spirit there should dwell in Him the same fullness; and as in the Son, the Father, and the Spirit were revealed, so in the Spirit are the Son and the Father made known in the soul."[2] As Jesus was Immanuel, *God with us,* the Holy Spirit is *God in us.*

Whatever God does, the entire Trinity does. The three Persons are one in being, in purpose, in activity. In Christian experience we know that we have to do, not with three Gods, but with the one true and living God.

[2]*The Way to Pentecost* (New York: Revell, 1940), p. 58.

Yet we participate in the one God through the special work of the Three. *Through* Christ we have access *in* the Holy Spirit *to* the Father (Eph. 2:18). To be Christian is to experience the three-one God.

b. The Persons of the Godhead. In thinking of the Trinity we must avoid the error that there are three beings—three individuals in the human sense—in the Godhead. This is the error of tritheism (three Gods) and is dangerously close to polytheism (many Gods).

Personality has two aspects—the individual and the social.[3] The *individual* aspect is that which sets one off as distinct from every other self. The *social* aspect is that which makes us a part of everyone else and prompts us to give ourselves to others in the fellowship of love.

Applying this to the "Persons" of the Godhead, we would say that each is distinct in one sense from the others but that each Person lives in and for the others. The three Persons of the Godhead are *distinct but not separate.* Each is in all, and all are in each. Thus God is not solitary but social in His being. The one God, who is holy love, is the perfect Pattern of all fellowship in love.

Dr. Chadwick points out: "The perplexity arises from our imperfect conception of the Persons of the Trinity. With us personality is divisive and exclusive. Each is separate from the rest and must always be a separate personality. Personality in the Trinity is not exclusive but inclusive, not divisive but inherent."[4]

3. *The Son and the Spirit.* In order to appreciate the full work of the Holy Spirit we need to understand the roles of Christ and of the Spirit.

a. Christ Came to Reveal God.

Philip voiced the deep yearning of the human heart when he asked the Saviour, "Shew us the Father." What is God like? What is He in His inmost heart?

[3]Conner, *op. cit.*, pp. 183-87.
[4]*Op. cit.*

The Old Testament gives us a gradual unfolding of God's self-disclosure. But God could not fully unveil himself to prophets or in parchments—*He must come to us in person.* So Jesus answered Philip, "He that hath seen me hath seen the Father" (John 14:9). Jesus was God clothed in human personality, that we might see Him and look upon Him, and handle Him—that we might *know* Him. In the words of the little child, "Jesus is the best picture God ever had took." Her grammar may have been atrocious, but her theology was apt. Since Jesus came, we know that our Father is a Christlike God.

The supreme and climactic revelation of God is in the cross and the resurrection of Christ. "Hereby perceive we the love of God, because he laid down his life for us" (I John 3:16). The Cross is the concrete expression of the holy love of God which takes up into itself the suffering and alienation of sin in order to destroy it—to make atonement.

In the cross of Christ I glory,
Tow'ring o'er the wrecks of time.
All the light of sacred story
Gathers round its head sublime.
—John Bowring

The Resurrection is the assurance of the divine victory over sin, death, and hell, and the pledge to us of a living Christ.

b. The Holy Spirit Came to Impart God.

The Holy Spirit came to apply to our hearts the benefits of Christ's redemptive sufferings. He exists to act *within.* "His it is to enter into the recesses of the human spirit and to work from within the subjectivity of man. From within our human being the Spirit vitalizes, stabilizes, renews, admonishes, warns, recalls, interprets, enlightens, guides, and gives comfort (or strength). He is God in His special activity and agency of secret invasion and invisible occupation."[5] He is the *sanctifying* Spirit—making us holy even as the Father is holy.

If God's self-revelation climaxed in Jesus' life, death, and resurrection, His self-impartation climaxed in His coming through the Spirit at Pentecost to indwell and sanctify His people. Jesus is God *with* us; the Holy Spirit is God *in* us.

C. The Comforter

One name given by Jesus to the Holy Spirit is *Comforter.* The Greek word Paraclete so translated means "one called to stand beside us." The exact English equivalent is the word *Advocate.* The Holy Spirit, Jesus promised, shall be with us—*in* us—to counsel us, to guide us, to help us, to console us in the dark night of suffering and sorrow.

Dr. G. Campbell Morgan and Dr. Samuel Chadwick were both speaking in a religious convention. In a message in the early part of a service Dr. Chadwick objected to the name Comforter for the Holy Spirit. He was arguing that the Spirit is our Advocate and he said he would never call his lawyer his comforter. Dr. Morgan followed on the program. He pointed out that he differed with his beloved friend, saying that if he needed a lawyer it would be a great comfort to know that his case was in the hands of an expert attorney. Many Christians are trying to live by their own wits and human resources, when they should have surrendered everything to the Holy Spirit. Oh, what rest when we cease from self and receive Him! When we "let go and let God"!

The English word "Comforter" comes from two words meaning "with strength." The Holy Spirit is our divine Strengthener and Helper. He is with us to give

[5]C. W. Lowry, *The Trinity and Christian Devotion* (New York: Harper and Brothers), p. 73.

wisdom, encouragement, and inspiration. And in the night of desolation He will cheer us with His warmth and love.

D. The Spirit of Christ

The distinctive teaching of the New Testament is that the Spirit of God is the Spirit of Christ. He is the Spirit of Christ because Christ was the Bearer and Baptizer with the Spirit. In the Book of Acts and in the Epistles of the New Testament the Spirit is called the Spirit of Jesus, the Spirit of Christ, the Spirit of Jesus Christ, and the Spirit of the Lord (or the Lord the Spirit).

1. *The Holy Spirit Is "Christ's Other Self."* To the disciples who were despondent at the thought of Jesus' departure from them the Saviour promised, "He shall give you *another* Comforter, that he may abide with you for ever . . . *I will not leave you orphans: I will come to you*" (John 14:16, 18, marginal reading). All that Christ had been to His disciples the Comforter was to be—and more. As long as Jesus was with them in the flesh, the Spirit was *with* them in His person; but Jesus promises, After My departure to the Father, He shall be *within* you. This is why He said, "It is expedient for you that I go away: for if I go not away, the Comforter will not come unto you; but if I depart, I will send him unto you" (John 16:7). In bestowing the Spirit, Christ was himself returning to dwell within their hearts. The indwelling Spirit is the indwelling Christ.

For this reason the New Testament speaks of the indwelling Presence sometimes as the Spirit, sometimes as Christ. Paul says in one place, "Christ liveth in me" (Gal. 2:20). In another place he speaks just as emphatically and tells us that we are the temples of the Holy Spirit (I Cor. 6:19). He prays for the Ephesians that *Christ* may dwell in their hearts and that they might be "filled with all the fulness of God" (Eph. 3:17-19). To the same readers he says, "Be filled with the *Spirit*" (Eph. 5:18; see Rom. 8:9-11).

There is no confusion of Persons in these passages. Christ, who is "the fulness of God," inhabits the temples of our hearts through the Spirit. There are two Persons but only one experience.

2. *The Holy Spirit Glorifies Christ.* There is about the Holy Spirit an "incurable tendency to self-effacement." Jesus said that He would not speak of himself, but rather, "He shall glorify me: for he shall receive of mine, and shall shew it unto you." As Christ came to glorify—reveal—the Father, the Spirit came to glorify Christ, that Christ may be "all, and in all."

To hold, as some do, that in regeneration we receive Christ and that in entire sanctification we receive the Holy Spirit is wrong for two reasons. First, it makes a false, unscriptural separation between Christ and the Spirit. Secondly, it overlooks the cardinal truth that the Holy Spirit comes to exalt and manifest Christ in our lives. To be filled with the Spirit is not simply to enjoy some mystical or emotional "experience"; it is to be invaded and possessed by the Spirit of Christ. There will be emotion, true enough, but emotion directed and controlled *toward Christlikeness.* The Corinthians thought that to be filled with the Spirit meant simply ecstasy; Paul informed them it meant to have divine love (I Cor. 13:1-7). The spiritual man, he said, has "the mind of Christ" (I Cor. 2:15-16). This is entire sanctification, for it is total sanctity.

3. *The Spirit of God Is the Spirit of Christ.* To the Romans, Paul wrote: "Ye are not in the flesh, but in the Spirit, if so be that the *Spirit of God* dwell in you. Now if any man have not the *Spirit of Christ,* he is none of his" (Rom. 8:9). The final proof that we know the in-

dwelling of the Spirit is that we manifest the spirit of Christ.

All that God does for us is to one end—that we might be able to confess with Paul: "I am crucified with Christ: nevertheless I live; yet not I, but Christ liveth in me: and the life which I now live in the flesh I live by the faith of the Son of God, who loved me, and gave himself for me" (Gal. 2:20).

As Christ came to be the perfect Pattern of the Spirit-filled life, when I am filled with the Spirit my life will flower with His gracious virtues—love, joy, peace, long-suffering, gentleness, goodness, faithfulness, meekness, self-control. "The fruits of the Spirit are the virtues of Christ." "Let this mind be in you which was also in Christ Jesus" (Phil. 2:5).

Luther said that if someone should knock at his door and ask, "Does Martin Luther live here?" he would answer, "Martin Luther used to live here, but he is dead. Jesus Christ lives here now!" T. O. Chisholm has voiced the yearning of every believer's heart:

Oh, to be like Thee! blessed Redeemer,
This is my constant longing and prayer.
Gladly I'll forfeit all of earth's treasures,
Jesus, Thy perfect likeness to wear.

Oh, to be like Thee! while I am pleading,
Pour out Thy Spirit, fill with Thy love;
Make me a temple meet for Thy dwelling,
Fit me for life and heaven above.

Oh, to be like Thee! Oh, to be like Thee!
Blessed Redeemer, pure as Thou art!
Come in Thy sweetness, come in Thy fullness;
Stamp Thine own image deep on my heart.

Questions for Discussion

1. Why is it important to stress the personality of the Holy Spirit?

2. What are our reasons for believing in the personality of the Spirit of God?

3. What do we mean by the "Persons" of the holy Trinity?

4. Explain the statement concerning the Persons of the Godhead: "Each is in all, and all are in each."

5. What is the distinct role of the Spirit in the work of God?

6. Explain the meaning of the title *Comforter* as applied to the Spirit.

7. Why is it important that we understand that the Spirit of God is the Spirit of Christ?

V

The Work of the Spirit

I believe in the infinite and eternal Spirit of God, equal with the Father and the Son, to be not only perfectly holy in himself, but the immediate cause of all holiness in us; enlightening our understandings, rectifying our wills and affections, renewing our natures, uniting our persons to Christ, assuring us of the adoption of sons, leading us in our actions, purifying and sanctifying our souls and bodies, to a full and eternal enjoyment of God.

—John Wesley

"Do it yourself" is fine until applied to religion. The majority of people today have developed their own religion, following in the footsteps of those men long ago who said, "Let us build us a city and a tower, whose top may reach unto heaven; and let us make us a name" (Gen. 11:4).

The Tower of Babel is a symbol of God's unequivocal condemnation of man's efforts to achieve his own salvation. The imagined self-sufficiency of the morally religious man is the most effective block to divine grace. To the "best" men of His day Jesus said, "The publicans and the harlots go into the kingdom of God before you." Not that God is indifferent to moral values, but He must teach man that he cannot save himself. All we can do for ourselves is refine our sin into self-righteousness—erect our own Towers of Babel. Therefore the first and most important lesson we must learn is that salvation is of *God.* "By grace are ye saved through faith; and that not of yourselves: it is the gift of God: not of works, lest any man should boast" (Eph. 2:8-9).

The doctrine of the Holy Spirit safeguards the priority of God in our redemption. *Redemption is of divine origin.* "Herein is love, not that we loved God, but that he loved us, and sent his Son to be the propitiation for our sins" (I John 4:10). Salvation is not the upward reach of man but the downward reach of God. "We love him, because he first loved us" (I John 4:19). *Our personal salvation is by divine initiative.* "Work out your own salvation with fear and trembling. For it is GOD which worketh in you both to will and to do of his good pleasure" (Phil. 2:12-13). We can work out our salvation because God is at work in us. The presence of the Spirit of God within our hearts is "the immediate cause of all holiness in us." This is what theologians call the prevenient grace of God—the grace which goes before and prepares the way for authentic salvation.

And every virtue we possess,
And every victory won,
And every thought of holiness
ARE HIS ALONE.

—HARRIET AUBER

From any point of view our salvation is but a response to God's prior love. It is God's gift and work, "that, according as it is written, He that glorieth, let him glory in the Lord" (I Cor. 1:31). God originates; we respond. God calls; we answer. God leads; we follow. Salvation is a *divine-human* encounter. To make it a human-divine relationship is to reenact Babel. "The Author of faith and salvation is God alone. It is he that works in us both to will and to do. He is the sole Giver of every good gift, and the sole Author of every good work. There is no more of power than of merit in man; but as all merit is in the Son of God, in what he has done and suffered for us, so all power is in the Spirit of God."[1]

[1]John Wesley, "A Farther Appeal to Men of Reason and Religion."

As the Holy Spirit is the *Author* of our holiness, so is He also the *Perfecter* of the holiness. Every stage of advancement in the Christian life is at His initiative. The Galatians had forgotten this all-important truth. "This only would I learn of you," Paul asks, "Received ye the Spirit by the works of the law, or by the hearing of faith? Are you so foolish? having begun in the Spirit, are ye now made perfect by the flesh?" (Gal. 3:2-3) If moment by moment we yield to His sanctifying influences, that good work which He has begun in us He will perform until the day of Jesus Christ. "The title 'holy,' applied to the Spirit of God, not only indicates that he is holy in his own nature, but that he makes us so; that he is the great fountain of holiness to his Church; the Spirit from whence flows all the grace and virtue, by which the stains of guilt are cleansed, and we are renewed in all holy dispositions, and again bear the image of our Creator."[2] Our total salvation is the work of the sanctifying Spirit.

A. The Holy Spirit and the Human Spirit

The writer was once dealing with a man about his personal relationship to God. The man made this statement: "When God gets ready to convert me, He will do so 'in the twinkling of an eye.'" He was immovable in this conviction. Shortly thereafter he died without being converted.

To acknowledge that our salvation is the work of the Spirit of God does not reduce man to an inanimate object like a stone or a stick. Although the Lord represents himself as the Potter, we are not passive lumps upon which He arbitrarily acts. To the prevenient grace of God is added the proclamation of the gospel. "So then faith cometh by hearing, and hearing by the word

[2]John Wesley, *Sermons*, "On Grieving the Holy Spirit," Introduction.

of God" (Rom. 10:17). God addresses us as free creatures capable of responding to His call.

Throughout the Bible we are challenged to *act*—to repent, to turn to God, to believe. "Choose you this day whom ye will serve" (Josh. 24:15). "To day if ye will hear his voice, harden not your hearts" (Ps. 95:7-8). "Come unto me, all ye that labour and are heavy laden, and I will give you rest" (Matt. 11:28). "If any man willeth to do his will, he shall know of the teaching" (John 7:17, ASV). Passages like these all point to the conclusion: "So then every one of us shall give account of himself to God" (Rom. 14:12). Being free, that is, we are accountable. Freedom is a fact of experience—without which there could be no moral life. Freedom may be so abused that we may "resist the Holy Ghost" (Acts 7:51). Hear the heartbroken sob of the Saviour over rebellious Zion: "O Jerusalem, Jerusalem, which killest the prophets, and stonest them that are sent unto thee; how often would I have gathered thy children together, as a hen doth gather her brood under her wings, and ye would not!" (Luke 13:34) The human will pitted against the divine!

Human freedom, however, operates only within the context of divine grace. We can seek God only when He is seeking us. "Seek ye the Lord while he may be found, call ye upon him while he is near" (Isa. 55:6). These words by Isaiah are echoed by Jesus, "No man can come to me, except the Father which hath sent me draw him" (John 6:44). Some wait for God to overwhelm them with irresistible grace—and procrastinate. Others vainly imagine they can call on God and be saved in the nick of time—and presume. The former error stems from an undue emphasis upon divine sovereignty; the latter arises from an unscriptural stress upon human freedom. Through the cross of Christ, God's grace is free *to* all and free *in* all; Christ's blood was shed for *every* man.

Nevertheless we must come to God in His time and on His terms.

B. The Preliminary Work of the Holy Spirit

Our salvation, we repeat, is wholly the work of God. God is the Author and Finisher of our faith. While we freely cooperate with Him to be saved, it is only by the strength of the grace He imparts to us by His Holy Spirit. He calls and we are awakened. He convicts and we confess our sins. He grants us repentance and we turn from our wicked ways. He promises pardon and we believe to the salvation of our souls. "The Author of faith and salvation is God alone."

1. *Awakening.* The drawing of our souls to God is the effect of the Spirit's magnetism. "The impulse to turn toward communion with God depends on the impact of divine agency upon the human spirit. This initial agency may be described by the term awakening, which thus denotes a pressure from the divine side which is unsought by men, but whose intent they can either follow or resist. Awakening is not so much regeneration as a preparation for the same."[3] Deeply we should sense that "the first wish to please God, the first dawn of light concerning his will, and the first slight transient conviction of having sinned against him" is the work of the Holy Spirit in His prevenient agency. Once we understand this we are forever prevented from the folly of boasting in ourselves.

2. *Conviction.* Awakened by the Spirit, we are soon led into a sense of guilt and condemnation because of our sin. Jesus clearly indicated that conviction was to be one of the offices of the Spirit during the Pentecostal era. "And he, when he is come, will convict the world in respect of sin, and of righteousness, and of judgment: of

[3]Sheldon, *Systematic Christian Doctrine*, p. 453.

sin, because they believe not on me; of righteousness, because I go to the Father, and ye behold me no more; of judgment, because the prince of this world hath been judged" (John 16:8-11, ASV). Under the impact of the Spirit's conviction we are made to see that sin is essentially the neglect of the Saviour and that righteousness is God's own gift bestowed through Christ—and further, that to go on in unbelief and sin is to suffer the final pronouncement of divine judgment which has already fallen upon Satan in the death of Christ on the Cross. In his sermon on the "Discoveries of Faith," Mr. Wesley says: "The Holy Spirit prepares us for his inward kingdom, by removing the veil from our heart, and enabling us to know ourselves as we are known of him; 'convincing us of sin,' of our evil nature, our evil tempers, and our evil words and actions; all of which cannot but partake of the corruption of the heart from which they spring. He then convinces us of the desert of our sins; so that our mouth is stopped, and we are constrained to plead guilty before God."

3. *Repentance.* As awakening leads to conviction, conviction leads to repentance. "For godly sorrow worketh repentance unto salvation, a repentance which bringeth no regret" (II Cor. 7:10, ASV). The apostle had not forgotten his own bitter experience as arch persecutor of the Church. Luke lifts the veil for us in his account of Saul's conversion. "And as he journeyed, he came near Damascus: and suddenly there shined round about him a light from heaven: and he fell to the earth, and heard a voice saying unto him, Saul, Saul, why persecutest thou me? And he said, Who art thou, Lord? And the Lord said, I am Jesus whom thou persecutest: *it is hard for thee to kick against the pricks*" (Acts 9:3-5). Saul had been kicking against the goads of divine conviction. Conviction and repentance are inseparably related as links in personal salvation. To the

convicted soul God grants repentance, but repentance is man's own free act.

There are two Greek words for *repentance* used by New Testament writers. One is a word which means mere regret. It is employed by Matthew with reference to Judas: "Then Judas, which had betrayed him, when he saw that he was condemned, *repented himself*, and brought again the thirty pieces of silver to the chief priests and elders, saying, I have sinned in that I have betrayed the innocent blood" (Matt 27:3-4). But Judas' "repentance" was really remorse: regret minus the hope of forgiveness. The word most frequently used in the New Testament means "a sincere and thorough change of the mind in regard to sin, involving a sense of personal guilt and a voluntary turning away from sin"—to God. "Let the wicked forsake his way, and the unrighteous man his thoughts: and let him return unto the Lord, and he will have mercy upon him; and to our God, for he will abundantly pardon" (Isa. 55:7). *Repentance is the return of the soul to God.* In reformation a man may "quit his meanness," but in repentance he forsakes his sins and comes home to God. Reformation is a moral act; repentance is a religious act. "The Spirit of God gives to all who will repent the gracious help of penitence of heart and hope of mercy, that they may believe unto pardon and spiritual life."[4]

4. *Saving Faith.* Repentance clears the way for justifying faith—puts us on believing ground. After warning the Pharisees that the publicans and harlots were entering the Kingdom before them, our Lord explained the reason: "For John came unto you in the way of righteousness, and ye believed him not: but the publicans and the harlots believed him; and ye, when ye had seen it, repented not afterward, *that ye might* believe

[4]*Manual,* Church of the Nazarene, "Articles of Faith," Article VIII.

him" (Matt. 21:32). Because they were impenitent the Pharisees could not believe—nor can we. Faith flowers only in a penitent heart. "A broken and a contrite heart, O God, thou wilt not despise."

In our misguided zeal we sometimes urge a person to "believe" when he has not fully repented. True enough, there are times when we should encourage the timid faith of the seeker; but we must make sure that all sin has been forsaken. *Generally, however, saving faith is the immediate gift of the Holy Spirit to a truly penitent seeker.* Such faith is the act of the whole man under the impact of the Holy Spirit and the word of the gospel. It is a living synthesis of belief, trust, and obedience. "For with the heart [the real self] man believeth unto righteousness; and with the mouth confession is made unto salvation" (Rom. 10:10). In a moment of reckless abandonment to God I let go, not only of my sins, but also of myself. I cast myself wholly on the mercy of God in Christ. "For by grace are ye saved through faith; and that not of yourselves: *it is the gift of God*" (Eph. 2:8).

5. *Conversion.* The Bible describes this turning of the soul from sin to salvation by the term conversion. We commonly use the word in a broader way to designate the first work of grace, but the Scriptures generally limit conversion to the human act in turning away from sin. Thus Jesus quoted the prophecy of Isaiah that "they should not see with their eyes, nor understand with their heart, and be converted, and I should heal them" (John 12:40). He also said, "Except ye be converted, and become as little children, ye shall not enter into the kingdom of heaven" (Matt. 18:3). Peter exhorted the people of Jerusalem, "Repent ye therefore, and be converted, that your sins may be blotted out" (Acts 3:19). Says Dr. H. Orton Wiley, "Through grace, preveniently bestowed, man turns to God and is then regenerated. Thus conversion in its truest scriptural meaning, is the

pivotal point, wherein through grace, the soul turns from sin, and to Christ, in order to regeneration."[5]

C. The Birth of the Spirit

Faith is the bridge over which the penitent believer passes from the death of sin to the life of God. All which precedes faith—awakening, conviction, repentance—is simply a clearing of the way for the soul to put its trust in Christ. *Faith alone brings pardon and new life.* Mr. Wesley says, "The very moment God giveth faith (for it *is* the gift of God) to the 'ungodly' that 'worketh not,' that 'faith is counted to him for righteousness.' "[6] "Therefore being justified by faith, we have peace with God through our Lord Jesus Christ" (Rom. 5:1).

1. *Justification and Regeneration.* The foregoing quotation from John Wesley is an account of justification. To be justified is to be pardoned from our sins and accounted as righteous in the sight of God. Justification means the restoration of a *right relationship with God.* How glorious to be forgiven! "Blessed are they whose iniquities are forgiven, and whose sins are covered. Blessed is the man to whom the Lord will not impute sin" (Rom. 4:7-8). But the instant God justifies He regenerates. "Regeneration, or the new birth, is that gracious work of God whereby the moral nature of the repentant believer is spiritually quickened and given a distinctively spiritual life, capable of faith, love, and obedience.[7] Justification is what God does *for* us through Christ; regeneration is what He does *in* us by the Holy Spirit.

2. *The New Birth.* Jesus said, "Except a man be born again, he cannot see the kingdom of God" (John

[5]*Christian Theology,* II, 378.

[6]*Sermons:* "Justification by Faith," IV, 4-6.

[7]*Manual,* Church of the Nazarene, "Articles of Faith," Article IX, par. 10.

3:3). Can original nature be changed? Of this the New Testament admits no doubt. We can become *new persons* by the power of God's Spirit! Old desires, old habits, old ways of living—these melt away as God breathes His Spirit within us. "If any man be in Christ, he is a new creature: old things are passed away; behold, all things are become new" (II Cor. 5:17). This is a miracle surpassing, say, the turning of water into wine. Dr. Arthur Gossip tells of an old Scotsman who had been wonderfully changed by the grace of God. He was so amazed at what God had wrought in his life he could not keep it to himself. One day some of his old friends decided they would mix him up on the Bible. "You surely don't believe that story about Jesus' turning water into wine, do you?" they jeered. "Well, I don't know that I can explain that," the old man answered, "but this I do know—at my house He turned beer into furniture."

Regeneration means the impartation of *a new mind*. "The natural man receiveth not the things of the Spirit of God: for they are foolishness unto him: neither can he know them, because they are spiritually discerned" (I Cor. 2:14). He can no more perceive the things of God than a man blind can enjoy the Swiss Alps or a deaf man can thrill to Handel's *Messiah*. Then he is born of the Spirit, and immediately his darkened mind is illuminated by the light of God! "For God, who commanded the light to shine out of darkness, hath shined in our hearts, to give the light of the knowledge of the glory of God in the face of Jesus Christ" (II Cor. 4:6). "The things of the Spirit of God" are no longer "foolishness unto him"—they are now as clear as day. "We have the mind of Christ."

Regeneration is the impartation of *new affections*. Jane was visiting her brother Jim at college. "Jim," she said, "before leaving I'd like to see your room in the dorm." "Aw, Sis," he protested, "you just think you want to see my room." But she insisted until he gave in.

As they entered the room Jane understood her brother's reluctance. Waiting a moment to gain her poise, Jane simply said, "Jim, I see you like pictures. If I sent you a picture, would you hang it on your wall?" He agreed he would. Several days later a package arrived from home. Jim eagerly opened it—a picture of *Christ!* As he held it against the wall, he knew that if he hung it there the other pictures would have to come down. And they did! That is a parable of what happens when Christ comes in. Sinful, worldly affections are canceled when Christ enters the heart. Thomas Chalmers called it "the expulsive power of a new affection." "Old things are passed away; behold, all things are become new."

Regeneration is the impartation of a *new will.* The essence of sin is the pleasing of self. "All we like sheep have gone astray; we have turned every one to his own way." We may go astray down different paths, but every sin is essentially an expression of self-will. To be born again is to be turned from the pleasing of self to the pleasing of God. Life is recentered in God under the impact of divine love. "For this is the love of God, that we keep his commandments: and his commandments are not grievous" (I John 5:3). "For the love of Christ constraineth us; because we thus judge, that if one died for all, then were all dead: and that he died for all, that they which live should not henceforth live unto themselves, but unto him which died for them, and rose again" (II Cor. 5:14-15).

Conversion is an outward thing; it means a turning around. I am facing one way—away from God; I turn around and face the other way—toward God. But the new birth is an inward thing; regeneration goes down to the very depths of my personality. It is a radical transformation of the innermost man, an impartation of new life, a new creation. People are converted differently, depending upon their background, temperament, and other factors. Some are converted quietly, like Lydia of

Thyatira, "whose heart the Lord opened" as the sunlight opens the rosebud. Others are converted by a cataclysm, like the jailer of Philippi. But regeneration always issues in the same thing: a life transformed in the image of God. "Now if any man have not the Spirit of Christ, he is none of his" (Rom. 8:9b).

3. *Regeneration and Sanctification.* Because regeneration means a new creation in Christ it may be truly called the beginning of sanctification. The new life principle imparted by the *Holy* Spirit is the principle of holiness. "The love of God is shed abroad in our hearts by the Holy Ghost which is given unto us" (Rom. 5:5). The New Testament therefore calls *all* believers "saints" or *holy ones.* The "washing of regeneration" (Titus 3:5) cleanses away the pollution of guilt acquired by sinful living. Writing to the Corinthian church Paul said, "Know ye not that the unrighteous shall not inherit the kingdom of God? Be not deceived: neither fornicators, nor idolaters, nor adulterers . . . shall inherit the kingdom of God. And such were some of you: but ye are *washed,* but ye are *sanctified,* but ye are *justified* in the name of the Lord Jesus, and by the Spirit of our God" (I Cor. 6:9-11). In his sermon on "Sin in Believers" John Wesley has an illuminating comment on this passage:

> "Ye are washed," says the apostle, "ye are sanctified;" namely, cleansed from "fornication, idolatry, drunkenness," and all other *outward* sin; and yet, at the same time, in another sense of the word, they were unsanctified; they were not washed, not *inwardly* cleansed from envy, evil surmising, partiality.[8]

Scripture, Christian experience, and the church creeds unite in the admission that original sin survives the new birth. The *reign* of sin is broken in regenera-

[8]See I Cor. 3:1-4.

tion, but the *remains* of sin are still there demanding a deeper purging. "I pray not for the world," says Jesus in His high priestly prayer, "but for them which thou hast given me . . . They are not of the world, even as I am not of the world. *Sanctify them*" (John 17:9, 16-17*a*). Sanctification at its deepest is the cleansing of the heart from the root of sin.

D. The Baptism of the Holy Spirit

Standing on the banks of the river Jordan, John the Baptist announced to the multitudes of Jerusalem: "I indeed baptize you with water unto repentance: but he that cometh after me is mightier than I, whose shoes I am not worthy to bear: he shall baptize you with the Holy Ghost, and with fire: whose fan is in his hand, and he will throughly purge his floor, and gather his wheat into the garner; but he will burn up the chaff with unquenchable fire" (Matt. 3:11-12). This glorious proclamation by John expresses the key promise of the new covenant—*the promise of heart cleansing.*

The words of John the Baptist indicate that the baptism with the Holy Spirit is a step beyond repentance and the moral adjustment of the new birth. To attempt to tie together the work of the Spirit in regeneration with that of His baptism as one work is such a strained assumption that we need not consider it. Birth precedes baptism—in the realm of the flesh and in the realm of the spirit. Each is complete and distinct within itself. Birth suggests the impartation of life; baptism connotes cleansing. It was to His disciples that Jesus applied the promise of John. A few moments before He went to the Father the Saviour assured the apostles: "John truly baptized with water; but ye shall be baptized with the Holy Ghost not many days hence" (Acts 1:5). That settles it—*the Spirit baptism is for the disciples of Christ.*

Not just for the apostles or the 120, but for us all. "For the promise is unto you, and to your children, and to all that are afar off, even as many as the Lord our God shall call" (Acts 2:39).

1. *To be baptized with the Holy Spirit is to be purified in heart.* At Pentecost the disciples of Christ were marvelously transformed from fearful, overly sensitive, selfish persons, to fearless, united, and Christlike witnesses. We have the circumstantial evidence in the Gospels and Acts, but we are not left to circumstantial evidence. Twenty years after Pentecost, Simon Peter is on the witness stand. Recounting his recent experience at the home of Cornelius, he says: "And God, which knoweth the hearts, bare them witness, giving them the Holy Ghost, even as he did unto us; and put no difference between us and them, *purifying their hearts by faith*" (Acts 15:8-9).

Here is a most significant and far-reaching scripture. Peter, telling of the incident at the home of Cornelius, tied this epochal incident into a parallel with the Day of Pentecost. In other words, he made it clear that God had put no difference between the Jew and the gentile, doing the same for one that He had performed for the other. The same witness that came on the Day of Pentecost came as well on the household of Cornelius. The same vital results appeared in the new gentile believers as had appeared in those Jews on the Day of Pentecost. And so Peter told exactly what had happened on the Day of Pentecost. What was it? ". . . purifying their hearts by faith."[9]

Peter makes no reference to the passing phenomena of Pentecost. Not a word concerning the wind, the fire, or the gift of languages. As meaningful as these symbols were, they were but passing manifestations of that hour.

[9]See H. V. Miller, *op. cit.*, pp. 17-18.

The permanent pattern for all time for Pentecost was purity of heart through the baptism with the Holy Spirit.

2. *To be baptized with the Holy Spirit is to be empowered.* "But ye shall receive power, when the Holy Spirit is come upon you: and ye shall be my witnesses . . ." (Acts 1:8, ASV). These words hark back to the promise of Jehovah given through Ezekiel: "I will put my spirit within you, *and cause you* to walk in my statutes" (Ezek. 36:27). Power for witnessing, power for life—the two are really inseparable. The full blessing of Pentecost is the sure way of becoming a blessing to others. "He that believeth on me," said Jesus, "from within him shall flow rivers of living water" (John 7:38, ASV). This He said of the Holy Spirit. A heart filled with the Spirit will overflow with the Spirit. It is not your power, but His power. "It is not abstract power under your control, but it is a Person, whose presence with you is necessary to your possessing and retaining the power. *He has the power and you have Him.*"[10] When He abides futility and failure are swallowed up by His glorious fullness.

3. *To be baptized with the Holy Spirit is to be stamped with the image of Christ.* Christ is himself the perfect Pattern of Pentecost. He is what man means by "God" and what God means by "man." He is the representation of the God who is and the man who is to be. To be baptized with the Holy Spirit is to have the sanctity and sanity of Jesus—to be saturated with His spirit.

The word translated "baptize" has among other meanings that of *dyeing* of cloth. It was a common household word. "What does dyeing imply?" Dr. H. V. Miller asks. "It means the saturating of that cloth with a distinct shade of coloring until every particle of the warp

[10]A. B. Simpson, *Power from on High* (Harrisburg, Pa.: Christian Publications), II, 78.

and woof was impregnated with that color. . . . And so it is. The baptism with the Holy Ghost by Jesus in the life of the believer who will have it so, is the actual saturating of that personality with divine presence until the very warp and woof of life takes on a divine cast."[11] Paul expressed it in these words: "But we all, with unveiled face beholding as in a mirror the glory of the Lord, are transformed into the same image from glory to glory, even as from the Lord the Spirit" (II Cor. 3:18, ASV). The baptism with the Holy Spirit means Christlikeness.

4. *To be baptized with the Holy Spirit is to be Spirit-filled.* "And when the day of Pentecost was fully come . . . they were all filled with the Holy Ghost" (Acts 2:1-4). Every born-again believer knows the Holy Spirit, but there is a precious fullness of the Spirit known only to those who have made a total surrender to Him. An illustration may help. Suppose an evangelist comes to a church to conduct a campaign. Arriving at the parsonage, he is greeted by the pastor and some of the church officials. They take him into the parsonage and show him the guest room he is to occupy. The pastor tells him to make himself perfectly at home. He may even raid the icebox at midnight if he gets hungry! Then suppose that several years later the pastor of that church moves to another field of labor. The congregation then extends a call to the man who had served them earlier as evangelist. Arriving at the same parsonage he is greeted by the same church officials, who welcome him, this time not as their evangelist, but as their pastor. Instead of showing him the guest room they hand him a ring of keys—keys to every door in the house. He is now to make his home in the parsonage.

To be born of the Spirit is a great miracle of grace.

[11]H. V. Miller, *op. cit.*, p. 13.

But how glorious to turn all the keys over to Him! The key to every secret closet where our fondest treasures are hid. The key to the attic of our imaginations. The key to the basement of our desires. The Spirit enters to possess the entire personality. He may rearrange the furniture of our lives as He chooses. He has come to *dwell* within the house of Man-soul! To yield ourselves up to Him in this way is to be *filled* with the Spirit.

Dr. E. Stanley Jones relates his own experience as follows: "I was a Christian for a year or more when one day I looked at a library shelf and was struck with the title of a book, *The Christian's Secret of a Happy Life.* As I read it my heart was set on fire to find this life of freedom and fullness. I reached page forty-two when the Inner Voice said very distinctly, 'Now is the time to find.' I pleaded that I did not know what I wanted, that when I finished it, I would seek. But the Inner Voice was imperious, 'Now is the time to seek.' I tried to read on, but the words seemed blurred. I was up against a divine insistence, so closed the book, dropped on my knees and asked. 'What shall I do?' The Voice replied, 'Will you give me your all—your very all?' After a moment's hesitation I replied, 'I will.' 'Then take my all, you are cleansed,' the Voice said with a strange, inviting firmness. 'I believe it,' I said and arose from my knees. I walked around the room affirming it over and over, and pushing my hands away from me as if to push away my doubt. This I did for ten minutes, when suddenly I was filled with a strange refining fire that seemed to course through every portion of my being in cleansing waves. It was all very quiet and I had hold of myself—and yet the divine waves could be felt from the inmost center of my being to my fingertips. My whole being was being fused into one, and through the whole there was a sense of sacredness and awe—and the most exquisite joy. Very emotional? So be it! But I knew then, and I know

now, that I was not being merely emotionally stirred, but the sources of my life were being cleansed and were taken possession of by Life itself. My will was just as much involved as my emotions. The fact is the whole of life was on a permanently higher level."[12]

Nor need you wait any longer. Our need is now. God's provision is now. We may have Him now if with all the heart we seek Him.

Hover o'er me, Holy Spirit;
Bathe my trembling heart and brow;
Fill me with Thy hallowed presence.
Come, oh, come and fill me now.

Questions for Discussion

1. Why is it important to understand that our salvation is the work of God?

2. What danger must we avoid in ascribing our personal salvation to the Holy Spirit?

3. Define prevenient grace and sketch the process.

4. At what stage does prevenient grace become saving grace?

5. Describe the birth of the Spirit.

6. Discuss the relationship between (a) justification and regeneration, (b) conversion and regeneration, (c) regeneration and sanctification.

7. Show by the Scriptures what is accomplished by the baptism with the Holy Spirit.

[12]*Victorious Living* (New York: The Abingdon Press), p. 120.

VI

The Dynamic of the Spirit

But ye shall receive power, after that the Holy Ghost is come upon you: and ye shall be witnesses unto me (Acts 1:8).

When D. L. Moody was preaching in Farewell Hall in Chicago, two humble Free Methodist women regularly attended his services. At the close of the meetings these women would say to Mr. Moody, "We are praying for you." He finally became somewhat nettled and said to them one night, "Why are you praying for me? Why don't you pray for the unsaved?" They replied, "We are praying that you may receive the power." Mr. Moody did not understand, but their words set him to thinking. He went to the women and said, "I wish you would tell me what you mean." Then they "expounded unto him the way of God more perfectly." At Mr. Moody's request these women and a few others began to meet each Friday afternoon at four o'clock to pray that their pastor would receive the baptism with the Holy Spirit. "Oh, how piteously I prayed that God might fill this empty vessel!" Mr. Moody himself later confessed. "After the fire in Chicago," he went on to relate, "I was in New York City, and going into the Bank on Wall Street, it seemed as if I felt a strange and mighty power coming over me. I went up to the hotel, and there in my room I wept before God, and cried, 'O, my God, stay Thy hand!' He gave me such a fullness that it seemed more than I could contain." This experience was the beginning of Mr. Moody's great success as a soul winner.

To the grieving disciples in the Upper Room, Jesus said, "It is expedient for you that I go away: for if I go not away, the Comforter will not come unto you; but if

I depart, I will send him unto you. And when he is come, he will reprove the world of sin, and of righteousness, and of judgment" (John 16:7-8). When the Spirit comes upon the Church in Pentecostal fullness, the world is convinced of its need. The coming of the Spirit at Pentecost marked more than the full sanctification of the individual disciples—it was the launching of God's D day for the redemption of the world. Pentecost initiated a new phase of the redemptive ministry of Christ. Consider two passages from the Fourth Gospel.

> *Sanctify them* . . . AS THOU HAST SENT ME INTO THE WORLD, EVEN SO HAVE I ALSO SENT THEM INTO THE WORLD. *And for their sakes I sanctify myself, that they also might be sanctified through the truth. . . . that the world may believe that thou hast sent me. . . . that the love wherewith thou hast loved me may be in them, and I in them* (John 17:17-19, 21, 26).

> *Then said Jesus to them again, Peace be unto you:* AS MY FATHER HATH SENT ME, EVEN SO SEND I YOU. *And when he had said this, he breathed on them, and said unto them, Receive ye the Holy Ghost* (John 20:21-22).

In both the prayer and the promise the theme is the same. The sanctification of the disciples and their reception of the Spirit are linked together with the Church's continuation of Christ's ministry to the world. Between Christ and His sanctified, Spirit-baptized Church there is an identity of mission. His disciples must carry forward the work which the Father had sent Him to earth to inaugurate. *"As my Father hath sent me, even so send I you"—Receive ye the Holy Spirit!* Understanding this perfectly, Luke prefaces the Book of Acts with a reference to his Gospel in these words: "The former treatise have I made, O Theophilus, of all that Jesus *began* both to do and teach" (Acts 1:1). The inference is irresistible that Jesus is to *continue* His ministry through His new body, the Church of Pentecost.

The Holy Spirit cleanses and fills the Church, not as a reservoir, but as a channel. Sanctification is not an end in itself; it is a means to a yet higher end. "Christianity that does not begin with the individual, does not begin; Christianity that ends with the individual—*ends!*" Christ baptizes us with His Spirit that we might become vessels "unto honour, sanctified, and meet for the master's use, and prepared unto every good work" (II Tim. 2:21). He does not sanctify us that we may enjoy a negative, static goodness; He purges us that we might become instruments of blessing. In *My Lady of the Chimney Corner,* Alexander Irvine tells of his Irish peasant mother, Anna. One day she went to comfort a sorrowing neighbor. "Now tell Him to lay His hand on your tired head in token that He's with you in your distress," Anna quietly counseled. The prayer was answered. The neighbor said she had received God's comfort, had felt a hand, "and the hand was just like yours, Anna." Anna replied, "Yes, the hand was mine, but it was God's, too." Sometimes, she said, God takes a bishop's hand, a doctor's hand, a mother's hand—"and sometimes He takes the hand of an old creature like me." *God purifies us from our selfishness that His love might move us to compassion.* For our sakes Christ dedicated himself to Calvary—that we might find our cross and give ourselves without measure for the salvation of the world. As there is a *human* consecration which precedes the work of entire sanctification, there is a *divine* consecration which follows.

From one standpoint the atonement is a finished work; once for all the Saviour suffered to put away sin by the sacrifice of himself. From yet another viewpoint the atonement is an ongoing process of reconciliation, carried forward by the Spirit within the Church. What else can the following passage mean? "And all things are of God, who hath reconciled us to himself by

Jesus Christ, and hath given to us the ministry of reconciliation; to wit, that God was in Christ, reconciling the world unto himself, not imputing their trespasses unto them; and hath committed unto us the word of reconciliation. Now then we are ambassadors for Christ, as though God did beseech you by us: we pray you in Christ's stead, be ye reconciled to God" (II Cor. 5:18-20). God's love, first manifested in Christ and His cross, was now incarnate in Paul. Jesus' prayer had been answered: "That the love wherewith thou hast loved me may be in them, and I in them." With complete candor and true humility the apostle could say, "I am crucified with Christ: nevertheless I live; yet not I, but *Christ liveth in me*" (Gal. 2:20). Paul had found an identity, not only of life but of mission, with Christ. So much so that he could write, "I Paul . . . now rejoice in my sufferings for you, and fill up that which is behind of the afflictions of Christ in my flesh" (Col. 1:23-24). *The atonement was moving forward through the sufferings of this Christ-indwelt man.* If we are to fulfill our ministry of reconciliation, to the passion of Christ we must add the compassion of our own hearts. This is possible only through the purging of Pentecost.

The baptism with the Holy Spirit is thus God's means of purifying and empowering the Church to carry forward the ministry begun by the Son. "But ye shall receive power, after that the Holy Ghost is come upon you: and ye shall be witnesses unto me both in Jerusalem, and in all Judaea, and in Samaria, and unto the uttermost part of the earth" (Acts 1:8). How can I claim to know the fullness of the Spirit if I am selfish and passionless? Only the passionate heart *is* pure.

A. The Empowerment of the Spirit

The Spirit baptism will not make all Christians evangelists. I may be as filled with the Spirit as Moody, or even Paul, but that will not make me a Moody or a Paul! But the baptism with the Spirit will make each one an influential witness for Christ in the field where God has called him to live and work. The Holy Spirit would anoint parents with power to set a godly example before their children and to train them for the service of God. He would anoint the Sunday school teacher with a compassionate heart and the power to lead the class to Christ. He would empower the Sunday school superintendent to be a valuable assistant to the pastor and a mighty man of God in overseeing that arm of the church which reaches out for a lost world. He would enable the young people's president to make the youth a spiritual force in the local church. He would unctionize the missionary president to inspire a vision and a passion for the lost of earth both far and near. He would anoint the official board to take their responsibility as under God, so that the pastor might be as free as possible to give himself to the ministry of the Word and prayer. The pastor, baptized with the Spirit, would preach with unction and power and care for the flock of God with a true shepherd's heart. The entire congregation would become a witnessing force in the community. When the elder Beecher was pastor of Park Street Church, Boston, someone asked him the secret of his success. His answer was, "I preach on Sunday, but I have 450 members who take my message on Monday and preach it wherever they go." Of the Early Church we read that "they were all filled with the Holy Ghost" and that "they that were scattered abroad went every where preaching the word." The Church universal, baptized with the Spirit, would be resistless in its influence and "terrible as an army with banners."

1. *The Power of Holy Character.* Fundamentally the power of the Holy Spirit is not to *do* but to *be.* The greatest sermons are those preached unconsciously.

Francis of Assisi invited one of his young friars to go to the city with him to preach. After transacting some business the two started back to the countryside. The friar turned to Francis and said, "I thought we were going to the city to *preach.*" *"We have been preaching,"* was the saint's unforgettable reply.

A faithful church member slipped away to be with Christ—quietly, as he had lived. He was a member of the church board but was unassuming and reserved. He taught a men's class who loved him as a brother and father. His home was open to the young people of the church, and frequently on weekends the young men from a nearby military base spent a night "at home away from home" with this fine Christian family. Though he was not a "prominent" man in the city, his passing was deeply felt. Hundreds thronged the home and the funeral parlor. Several sons and a son-in-law were moved to surrender their lives to Christ before the funeral service. The church was filled to capacity for that service. *A man of God had died.* Who can estimate the power of such a life? Skeptics may answer many of our arguments; they cannot answer a holy life. *Holiness* remains the first work of the *Holy* Spirit.

2. *The Power of Love.* "The love of God is shed abroad in our hearts by the Holy Ghost which is given unto us" (Rom. 5:5). Commissioner Brengle tells how "on January 9th, 1885, at about nine o'clock in the morning, God sanctified my soul. It was a Heaven of love that came into my heart. I walked out over Boston Common before breakfast, weeping for joy and praising God. Oh, how I loved! In that hour I knew Jesus, and I loved Him till it seemed my heart would break in love. I loved the sparrows, I loved the dogs, I loved the horses, I loved the little urchins on the streets, I loved the strangers who hurried past me, I loved the heathen

—I loved the whole world."[1] Such ecstasy of course soon subsides into "a calm and peaceful love," but the heart of the holiness imparted by the Spirit is holy *love*. Such love is irresistible and irrepressible—it is the motive power back of all effective work for Christ. Without this love all our gifts are but as "sounding brass, or a tinkling cymbal." But clothed in that love the man with but little talent often becomes a wonder of power.

"I had an ignorant man in my church in Philadelphia," said Dr. J. Wilbur Chapman, "who utterly murdered the king's English. When he first stood up to talk, and you heard him for the first time, you would be amazed, and would hope that he would not speak long. But soon you would begin to wonder at the marvelous power of his words. I will tell you the secret of it. I once called thirty of the workers of my church together to pray for the baptism of power for special work. He rose and left the room. I afterward found him alone in a little room of the church pleading in prayer: 'O Lord, take all sin from me. Teach me what it is that hinders Thy coming. I will give up everything. Come, O Holy Spirit, come and take possession of me, and help me to win men.' He arose from his knees and met me face to face, and said, 'Pastor, I have received the Holy Ghost.' " Within three years he led a hundred men to Christ.[2]

3. *The Power of a Person.* Actually this humble man of whom Dr. Chapman tells was wiser than his pastor. It is a mistake to seek power as such. Power is the by-product of purity and of the Spirit's indwelling. "He has the power, and you have Him." Or better, *He has you.* "When we know that we have within us the indwelling presence of God, we become at once partakers of His omnipotence."[3]

[1]*Helps to Holiness,* ix.

[2]A. M. Hills, *Holiness and Power,* pp. 329-30.

[3]A. B. Simpson, *op. cit.,* p. 115.

Dr. J. Wilbur Chapman came himself into a new relationship with God while still in Philadelphia. At a conference at Northfield, Massachusetts, he was invited by Dr. F. B. Meyer to speak. Much to Dr. Meyer's surprise Chapman said:

> "Some years ago when I was the minister of the Wanamaker Church in Philadelphia I found myself breaking under the strain of the work. I had given all my energy to it, but it availed little and on a Monday morning, utterly discouraged, I wrote my resignation to the church officials. While the ink was still wet on the paper the morning 'Tribune' was passed into my study. I opened it up and on an inside page read the report of a sermon by Dr. Meyer which he had delivered the previous day at Northfield. The keynote of the sermon was this: Many ministers and Christian workers are breaking down working for God instead of yielding themselves to God so that He may work through them. I was convinced at once," he added, "and tore up my resignation and prayed, 'God forgive me for forgetting Thee. Send the rivers of Thy power flowing through me.'"[4]

That was the turning point in the great evangelist's ministry. The inrush of the Holy Spirit lifts life out of the shallows into the mighty, oceanic fullness of God. "Ye shall receive power, after that the Holy Ghost is come upon you." When He has come to dwell within, we are enabled to work and to witness, to live and to serve—*"not somehow, but triumphantly!"*

Paul speaks of "the supply of the Spirit of Jesus Christ" (Phil. 1:19). It is as though we were connected up with the Dynamo of the universe. The power of the Holy Spirit is not stored up in our little batteries —it flows in and through us as we maintain constant contact with God. In order to retain the dynamic of the Spirit we must continue to meet the conditions of

[4]Quoted by J. S. Bonnell, *Psychology for Pastor and People* (New York: Harper and Brothers), pp. 62-63.

obedience and *trust.* We can have His power only in the line of His will. The electric train can draw the power from the wire only insofar as it follows the track. It can have the power to run along the rails, but it cannot have it to run into the neighboring farms and follow the capricious will of the engineer. The Holy Ghost is given to them that obey Him (Acts 5:32). This obedience is a much larger thing than we sometimes imagine. "It is not merely to keep from doing wrong in some little contracted sphere; but it is to understand and follow the whole will and purpose of God in the use of this divine enduement. We cannot have it to please ourselves. We cannot have it to please ourselves even in the mode of our Christian work. *We can only enjoy the fullness of the Spirit, in so far as we use this fullness for the work to which He has called us.*"[5]

And to what work has God commissioned the Church? "Ye shall be witnesses unto me both in Jerusalem, and in all Judaea, and in Samaria, and unto the uttermost part of the earth." We can know the fullness of the Spirit's power only as we use it to give the gospel to the whole world. "Only in the line of the world's evangelism and the fulfillment of our great trust can the church of God ever realize the utmost meaning of the promise of Pentecost."[6]

Lead on, O King Eternal. The day of march has come;
Henceforth in fields of conquest Thy tents shall be our home.
Thro' days of preparation Thy grace has made us strong;
And now, O King Eternal, we lift our battle song.

—Ernest W. Shurtleff

[5]Simpson, *op. cit.,* p. 79.
[6]*Ibid.*

B. How to Enter In

As we study the deeper experiences of great Christians we are impressed with the beautiful variety of God's dealings with men. There certainly is no uniform pattern to be found, although certain underlying principles are apparent in every instance where the Holy Spirit has come in His sanctifying fullness. But there is no quick and easy formula for the power of God; *God cannot be manipulated by psychological technique.*

Nevertheless, certain conditions must exist before we can enter into the precious experience of full salvation. The suggestions that follow in this chapter are not to be understood necessarily as rungs of a ladder, or even in every instance as conscious steps which one takes as he seeks to be filled with the Spirit. They are to be considered rather as *underlying conditions which must prevail* before we know the Holy Spirit in His sanctifying power.

1. *I must be in a state of conscious acceptance with God before I can be filled with the Spirit.* In His instructions to His disciples Jesus made it clear that His gift of the Comforter was not for the world but for the Church. "If ye love me, keep my commandments. And I will pray the Father, and he shall give you another Comforter, that he may abide with you for ever; even the Spirit of truth; *whom the world cannot receive,* because it seeth him not, neither knoweth him: but ye know him; for he dwelleth with you, and shall be in you." Here is promised a gift of the Spirit to those who are already acquainted with Him.

Believers know the Holy Spirit is with them. He disturbs them by flashes of insight, by touching them here and there. But all this is "with" and not "in." "He goads us rather than guides us, illuminates rather than invigorates, prods us into activity rather than penetrates all activities—it is from without in, instead of within out." Pentecost means the Holy Spirit dwelling *within* as the Source of our very life. But He must be "with" us before He can be "in" us.

This deeper experience of the Spirit, that is, is reserved for those who are already acquainted with Him by way of the new birth. *Seekers after "the fullness of the blessing" are sometimes disillusioned later because what they found was not the Holy Spirit in sancitfying power, as they supposed, but simply a restoration of their fellowship with God.* Only those who know themselves fully forgiven and in a clear state of regeneration are on grounds to be baptized with the Spirit. Many Christians are living on a plane lower than the point where sanctification begins. The fullness of the Spirit is for those who are happily walking in the light!

2. *Only those who have an intense spiritual thirst are filled with the Spirit.* "Now on the last day, the great day of the feast, Jesus stood and cried, saying, If any man *thirst*, let him come unto me and drink. He that believeth on me, as the scripture hath said, from within him shall flow rivers of living water. But this spake he of the Spirit, which they that believed on him were to receive: for the Spirit was not yet given; because Jesus was not yet glorified" (John 7:37-39, ASV). We are reminded of the prophecy of Isaiah: "For I will pour water upon him that is *thirsty*, and floods upon the dry ground: I will pour my spirit upon thy seed, and my blessing upon thine offspring" (Isa. 44:3).

In the same vein Jesus said, "Blessed are they which do *hunger* and *thirst* after righteousness: for they shall be filled" (Matt. 5:6). Yes, the Spirit is bestowed "upon him that is *thirsty*." "Oh, how piteously I prayed," Moody testified, "that God might fill this empty vessel!" When a man really thirsts, every pore of his body seems to cry, "Water! Water! Water!" When a man thirsts spiritually, his whole being cries out. "As the hart panteth after the water brooks, so panteth my soul after thee, O God. My soul thirsteth for God, for the living God." *Come, Holy Spirit, come!* Nothing short of an all-absorbing desire will bring the Spirit. Dr. R. A. Torrey was to speak at Northfield at one of Mr. Moody's conferences. His announced subject for that Sunday morning was "The Baptism with the Holy Spirit, How to Get It." Early that morning a minister who had come all the way from New Jersey for the purpose of being baptized with the Spirit came to see Mr. Torrey in person. He said, *"I would rather die than go back to my church without it."* Mr. Torrey answered, "My brother, you are going to have it." On Monday morning before returning to New Jersey he paid a parting visit to Mr. Torrey, and said, "I want to tell you I have received the baptism with the Holy Spirit."[7]

3. *I must be fully surrendered and abandoned to the will of God.* This abandonment has been termed consecration and the death to self. But whatever our terminology, we must come to the crisis of self-abandonment to the will of God. The crisis comes only after we have become painfully aware of our deep self-centeredness and double-mindedness. The crisis of the new birth brings release from festering sins and marks the introduction of a new life. Regeneration is a glorious release, but not a full release. Festering sins are gone, but the roots of the disease are still there. The new life is introduced, but is not fully regnant. The old life is subdued, but not surrendered. The Christian who takes seriously the call to holiness cannot be satisfied with this double-minded condition. He hungers and thirsts after righteousness. He must bring the matter to a *crisis* through an abandonment of himself to God. Consecration moves on a deeper level than the initial surrender

[7]R. A. Torrey, *The Holy Spirit* (New York: Revell), pp. 177-78.

to Christ for pardon. Its motivation is a deepened conviction of the pervasive nature of self-will. It is the frank and contrite acknowledgment of one's pettiness, ambition, pride, and selfishness, and a conscious, willing commitment of the self in love to God.

Such a consecration is not simply a general prayer, but a heart plea which will not be hushed until the inner self can wholeheartedly respond to the faintest whisper of God. Dr. E. Stanley Jones has said:

> There is no love between persons unless there is mutual self-surrender. If either withholds the inmost self love is blocked. So here.

He goes on to say:

> Then pay the price of a complete surrender. I mean surrender and not dedication. In dedication you still have your hands on the gift—in surrender you let go. The gift doesn't belong to you any more—it totally and wholly belongs to Another. You now lead a Spirit-led life, instead of a self-led life. You substitute One Will for two wills. You say to yourself, "Let go, let God."
>
> You put yourself at the disposal of the Divine. You surrender for better or for worse, for riches or for poverty, in sickness and in health, in life and in death—you will keep yourself only unto Him. *He has you.*[8]

This surrender is both implicit and explicit. It includes the surrender of the total self and of every idol of the heart, however small. The sainted Fenelon said trenchantly: " 'That's nothing,' we say. Yes, it is nothing, but a nothing which is all for you, a nothing which you care enough for to refuse it to God; a nothing which you scorn in words so that you may have an excuse to refuse it, but at bottom, it is a nothing which you are keeping back from God, and which will be your undoing."[9] Consecration for holiness has therefore been called the death to self. "I died and I died ungraciously,

[8]*Abundant Living* (New York: Abingdon), p. 157.

[9]*Christian Perfection* (New York: Harper and Brothers), p. 36.

but I died to nothing but that which caused me to die," is the witness of Rufus Moseley. This death is the gateway to the Spirit-filled life.

Uncle Bud Robinson heard Dr. W. B. Godbey preach on holiness in Alvarado, Texas. "After listening awhile," Bud relates, "I said, 'This is the best religion I ever heard a man preach, but a man could not get it.'" For the next four years he was a constant seeker after the fullness of the Spirit. In 1889 Bud began preaching the gospel. He sought and preached entire sanctification until in 1890 one summer Sunday morning he took for his text, "The very God of peace sanctify you wholly."

"I preached the best I could on holiness as the second definite work of grace, and told the people I didn't have it, but that I wanted it and was going to have it at any cost."

That night he preached at another appointment some six miles away on the text, "Follow peace with all men, and holiness, without which no man shall see the Lord." When he finished his message, he said, "We are going to have at least one seeker after this experience, and that is going to be me." True to his word, he knelt at the altar and began seeking heart holiness. That night F. M. McNary, a Presbyterian elder, also knelt by Uncle Bud's side and together they sought the fullness.

On the following day Uncle Bud returned to his little farm, where he was thinning corn. Finally, under deep conviction for the experience, he fell on his knees between two rows of corn. Here he really began to consecrate his all to God.

"At length God began to kindle the fire in my heart. Anger boiled up and God skimmed it off, and pride boiled up and God skimmed it off, and envy boiled up and God skimmed it off, until it seemed to me that my heart was perfectly empty. I said, 'Lord, there won't be anything left in me.' God seemed to say, 'There will be some left, but there will not be much left, but what little there is will be clean.'

"When my heart was empty a river of peace broke loose in the clouds. It flowed into my empty heart until a few moments later my heart was full and overflowing, and the weight of heaven became so great and grand and glorious that it seemed that I would die if God did not stay His hand."[10]

4. *I must appropriate the Holy Spirit by faith.* Faith is the hand of the heart which receives the promised gift of the Spirit. When our surrender is complete, faith usually is spontaneous, but entire sanctification is more than consecration. Consecration is the human act; sanctification is the divine response—and faith is the link between the two. "That the offering up of the Gentiles might be accpetable, being sanctified by the Holy Ghost" (Rom. 15:16*b*).

Said Jesus: "If ye then, being evil, know how to give good gifts unto your children: how much more shall your heavenly Father *give* the Holy Spirit to them that ask him?" (Luke 11:13) A fine Christian lady had gone to the altar repeatedly to be sanctified, but she could never seemingly break through to a satisfying experience. Well-meaning people would counsel her by asking, "You are all on the altar, aren't you?" "Yes," she would answer—but she never struck reality. Then her pastor was enabled to guide her to exercise appropriating faith. Her heart responded—*the Spirit came!* Her life was transformed by a new radiance. At once she became a new spiritual force in the church. To receive the Spirit we must exercise a childlike faith which appropriates the gift.

"But what is that faith whereby we are sanctified, —saved from all sin and perfected in love?" Mr. Wesley

[10]*Holiness in Doctrine and Experience* (Kansas City: Nazarene), pp. 113-14.

asks. "It is a divine evidence and conviction, *first,* that God hath promised it in the holy Scripture." As Hebrews puts it, "He that cometh to God must believe that he is, and that he is a rewarder of them that diligently seek him" (Heb. 11:6). "It is a divine evidence and conviction, *secondly,* that what God hath promised He is able to perform. . . . It is, *thirdly,* a divine evidence and conviction that He is able and willing to do it now. And why not? Is not a moment to Him the same as a thousand years? He cannot want more time to accomplish whatever is His will. And He cannot want or stay for any more *worthiness* or *fitness* in the persons He is pleased to honour. . . . To this conviction, that God is both able and willing to sanctify us now, there needs to be added one thing more,—*a divine evidence and conviction that he doeth it* . . . If you seek it by faith, you may expect it *as you are;* and if as you are, then expect it now. . . . Expect it by faith; expect it *as you are;* and expect it *now.*"[11]

In the Gospel of Mark we find an amazing statement by Jesus: "Therefore I say unto you, All things whatsoever ye pray and ask for, *believe that ye receive them,* and ye shall have them" (Mark 11:24, ASV). Preaching on appropriating faith, a minister told how as a small lad Christmas usually meant only a stocking of candy, nuts, and fruit. How he longed for a little red wagon! Then one autumn the boy's father said to him, "Come Christmas, Son, and you will have a red wagon like you've always wanted!" The boy knew his father to be a man of his word—*the promise was as good as the wagon.* One day late in October an adult neighbor noticed the lad strangely pulling some imaginary object about the yard. "What on earth are you doing, Buddy?" he asked. *"I'm pulling my red wagon!"* was the assured answer of the child. And come Christmas, he had his red

[11]*Sermons,* "The Scripture Way of Salvation," Vol. II.

wagon. In asking the Father for the gift of the Spirit we must exercise the same childlike faith.

If our faith were but more simple,
We would take Him at His word,
And our lives would be all sunshine
In the sweetness of our Lord!
—F. W. Faber

So Paul counsels us: "Likewise reckon ye also yourselves *to be* dead indeed unto sin, but alive unto God through Jesus Christ our Lord" (Rom. 6:11). *Faith reckons as accomplished fact what God has promised.* That is, when surrender is absolute and complete.

On an Indian mission station preparations were being made for a visit of the provincial governor to the school. The missionary who was doing most of the preparing was inwardly setting her house in order to receive the Divine Guest, the Spirit. Her heart was panting after the Spirit as the hart panteth for the water brooks. Another missionary was standing on the veranda watching for the governor to come around the hill. When he did so, the watchman called to those in the house, "He has come." The lady, whose deepest undertone was this craving for the Spirit, thought for the moment that the announcement was that the Spirit had come. Her faith at that moment closed the circuit. He *had* come! She went quietly into her room, closed the door, and knelt and thanked God that He had come. When she came out to meet the governor there was a new sparkle in her eyes and a radiance of countenance that does not come from merely meeting a governor!

Lord, I am waiting at Thy feet,
My consecration is complete;
Nothing from Thee would I withhold.
Let me Thy glorious face behold.

Weary of battles fought within,
Save me and cleanse me from all sin.
This is my longing, my desire;
Come, Thou refining, cleansing Fire.

Emptied of self and filled with Thee,
Spirit of God, abide with me.
Help me to die to self and sin;
Spirit divine, come in, come in!

—HALDOR LILLENAS[12]

Questions for Discussion

1. Why is it important that we understand Pentecost as more than an experience of individual cleansing from sin?

2. What is the significance of the claim, "The Spirit baptism will not make all Christians evangelists"?

3. What is involved in the empowerment of the Holy Spirit?

4. What lessons do Christian workers need to learn from the experience of Dr. J. Wilbur Chapman at Wanamaker Church?

5. What dangers must we avoid in speaking of the "technique" of receiving the Holy Spirit?

6. Discuss the underlying conditions one must meet to be Spirit-filled.

7. Discuss faith as the indispensable condition of receiving the gift of the Spirit.

[12]Copyright by Lillenas Publishing Company. Used by permission.

Printed in the United States
17378LVS00005B/1-138

9 780834 121447